One Man's Dream

The story behind G. Stuart Ogilvie

and the creation of

Thorpeness

Ailsa Ogilvie de Mille

NOSTALGIA
Publications

TOFTWOOD · DEREHAM · NORFOLK

To G. Stuart Ogilvie
– whose dream came true

Published by:

NOSTALGIA
Publications

(Terry Davy)
7 Elm Park, Toftwood,
Dereham, Norfolk NR19 1NB

First Impression 1996

© Nostalgia Publications 1996

ISBN 0 947630 15 5

Design and Typesetting:
NOSTALGIA PUBLICATIONS

Printed by:
COLOURPRINT
Fakenham, Norfolk

Contents

Acknowledgements

I would like particularly to thank Glen Ogilvie for allowing me to have the family archives, including Minute Books, "The Book", photograph and cuttings books and various papers covering the years from G. Stuart Ogilvie's inheritance until his death in 1932, and A. Stuart's death in 1972.

Also thanks to those - now no longer with us - who worked on the estate during this time, for their help in the 1970's in recounting and letting me take down their memories. In particular to the late Graeme Kemp for the happy hours I spent with him, learning not only of his work but that of his father and grandfather before him. His lively reminiscences and comments and the kind loan of his papers and photographs have been invaluable.

Likewise my thanks to the late "Hoppy" Cooper whose vivid memories have added colour to my story, and those of Micky Staff, Julia Woolnough, Roberta Meadows, Percy Westrup, Nellie Webster and others who remembered Margaret Ogilvie in her old age and the old hamlet of Thorpe.

My thanks also to the Ipswich and Suffolk Records Office for their help in my research in studying old newspapers, maps, books and other written evidence. Also all those still living (or only recently deceased) who have added to my knowledge of their memories and views on these difficult years of struggle, hey-day and change.

Finally, my thanks to Jo Vallance for all her typing assistance, and above all for her enthusiasm and support throughout this project; also to my granddaughter, Katy Prickett, for her invaluable help with the final preparation for publication.

Introduction

THORPENESS is different. No imposing hotels. No rows of Victorian or Edwardian boarding-houses. Those looking for a promenade or esplanade look in vain. In fact, the black and white houses on the main curved road overlooking a common have a faintly Tudor feel with their beams, while the little street of West Gate is positively medieval and slightly foreign. The atmosphere of unhurried tranquillity is added to by the fact that no two houses are exactly the same and every house is set in its own little cottage garden. As for the much-photographed "House in the Clouds", it is a disguised water tower built like a giant dovecote, with a five-storey house in its stalk - (and designed like this from the start and not an added afterthought).

Visitors to Thorpeness find it hard to believe that this picturesque garden village two miles north of Aldeburgh was, as recently as 1910, without a single tree. Nothing used to shield the various little dwellings scattered among the sand-dunes from the windswept shore and wild open heathland which surrounded them. Meanwhile, the boggy tidal fen, fed by the little River Hundred in the west, was joined by the salt waters swirling in and out with the tide from the estuary at Thorpe Haven. Storms, floods, erosion and silting up were frequent occurrences. Life in Thorpe could be harsh.

Today it is a Conservation Village and registered as an Area of Outstanding Natural Beauty. It is famous for its beautiful Meare - sixty-two acres of shallow interlinking lakes and waterways, set with tree-covered islands with enchanting little pavilions bearing names like "The Brigands' Haunt", "The Pirates' Lair", or "Wendy's House". One is staggered at the thought of it being man-made and literally dug out by hand and also that the whole idea and development was the creation of one mind - one man - G. Stuart Ogilvie. The story of How, Why and When and the difficulties he encountered is now fascinating history, and I have constantly been asked to write it down - and also perhaps to counter some of the strange myths which always grow up where facts are not known.

As the granddaughter of this remarkable man, I spent the early years of my life in his house and have always had close links with the estate. I have also been privileged, by courtesy of the present heir, Glen Ogilvie, to see all the papers and records of the growing village from its inception. Added to which, I was fortunate enough to be able, in the 1970's and 1980's, to take verbal records of this exciting time from a number of the key figures (since deceased) who had helped in its development. In particular, the late Graeme Kemp, who was Works Manager from the very beginning and responsible for the making of "the Meare."

Earnest gentlemen (and some ladies) have already written many articles or chapters in books about Thorpeness because it was a "purpose-built" village and entirely the creation of that one single man. They make assumptions as to how and why it was built, and point out various "influences" of contemporary architects and other "model villages" (many, like Portmeirion, not even thought of then), or "the trend" for seaside developments around the turn of the century. However, nothing could be further from the truth than their "logical conclusions." It was also assumed that G. Stuart Ogilvie was so rich that money was no problem, whereas battling with overdrafts and obtaining finance was in fact a constant struggle.

First, however, a word about G. Stuart Ogilvie himself and how - against all odds - he found himself, at the age of fifty, heir to the family estate.

Ailsa deMille

Four generations of the Ogilvie family

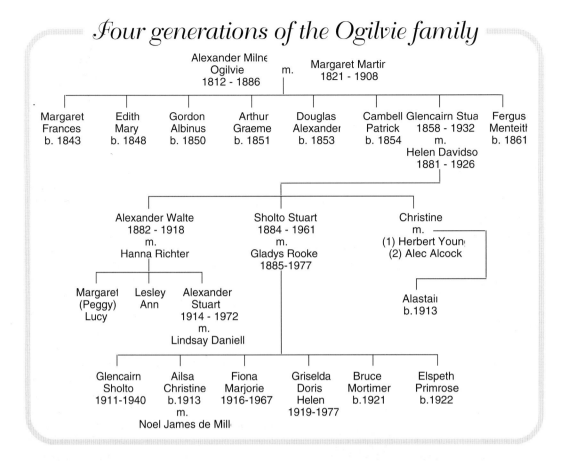

Alexander Milne Ogilvie 1812 - 1886 **m.** Margaret Martin 1821 - 1908

- Margaret Frances b. 1843
- Edith Mary b. 1848
- Gordon Albinus b. 1850
- Arthur Graeme b. 1851
- Douglas Alexander b. 1853
- Cambell Patrick b. 1854
- Glencairn Stuart 1858 - 1932 **m.** Helen Davidson 1881 - 1926
- Fergus Menteith b. 1861

Alexander Walter 1882 - 1918 **m.** Hanna Richter

Sholto Stuart 1884 - 1961 **m.** Gladys Rooke 1885-1977

Christine **m.** (1) Herbert Young (2) Alec Alcock

- Margaret (Peggy) Lucy
- Lesley Ann
- Alexander Stuart 1914 - 1972 **m.** Lindsay Daniell

Alastair b.1913

- Glencairn Sholto 1911-1940
- Ailsa Christine b.1913 **m.** Noel James de Mill
- Fiona Marjorie 1916-1967
- Griselda Doris Helen 1919-1977
- Bruce Mortimer b.1921
- Elspeth Primrose b.1922

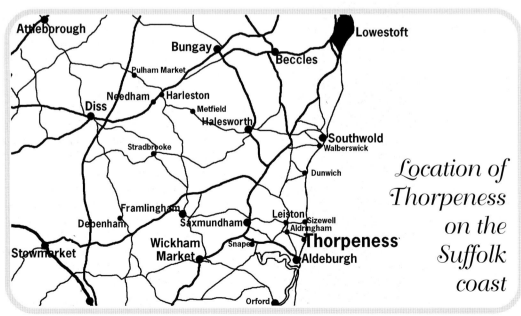

Location of Thorpeness on the Suffolk coast

6

Chapter One

G. Stuart Ogilvie

GLENCAIRN Stuart Ogilvie (always called Stuart) was the fifth son out of six of the eight children of Alexander - a Civil Engineer (privately educated and Edinburgh University) who had made a fortune as a railway pioneer - and Margaret (née Martin), of Sizewell House, Suffolk. As such, Stuart never expected to inherit the Sizewell estate which the family had built up over the years since purchasing the original small holiday home and two and a half acres in 1859. However, due to unexpected deaths and tragedies in the family, upon the demise of his eighty-six year old mother in 1908, it fell to him. It was by then of considerable size - over 6,000 acres - with many farms, arable and pasture

*G. Stuart Ogilvie
at Sizewell Hall
in 1917*

land, marshes and dry heaths, and seven miles of coast from Dunwich in the north to Thorpe in the south. Stuart was already fifty years old.

G. Stuart, as he signed himself, was educated at Rugby and University College, Oxford. He was called to the bar at the Inner Temple in 1882. He never practised law, however, as, while he was still at Oxford, he had a play produced in London. Stage-struck, he was determined to be a playwright and writer. He was successful, and at one time had three plays on at once. His dramatisation of Kingsley's 'Hypatia' at the Haymarket (his favourite theatre) ran longer than any other previous London play. Well-known artistes took leading parts in his productions, and Sir Henry Irving (the first actor to be knighted) became a lifelong friend and frequent visitor. Many people suggested that Stuart, himself, should take up acting. He was a larger than life character, six foot three with striking looks and a great sense of drama. He preferred, however, to let his imagination run and to create the dramatic situations and scenes and then watch them acted out.

He had married in 1881 Helen Davidson, the daughter of a London solicitor with a house in Aldeburgh. Septimus Davidson had caused quite a drama himself in 1862 when, as a keen amateur archaeologist, he discovered the first Anglo-Saxon Ship Burial at Snape (the contents of which are in the British Museum). The young Ogilvie couple had two sons and a daughter. Once they had taken possession of the estate, Stuart modernised and enlarged the house and redesigned the extensive grounds. Landscape gardening was his great hobby. As can still be discerned in the Thorpeness of today, he always included vistas, gazebos, dovecotes, surprises, large lawns and a lake or a pond "- water, the other dimension" he called it. He wasted no time, and engaged twenty gardeners and tree-planters, and included a small lake and many summer houses.

By 1910, the farms were progressing well under his mother's old farm manager, Harry Kemp, and his gardens under Harry's surveyor son, Graeme. Now that the house and gardens were greatly enlarged, Stuart changed the name to Sizewell Hall and began to look around with closer interest at other areas of his property: particularly the little fishing hamlet of Thorpe which lay on his southern boundary. He had always been fond of this - to many - rather bleak little settlement scattered between the windswept

almost to the foothill of Aldeburgh Church. His neighbouring landowner, however, had then stopped up the entrance and drained the land for pasture.

Stuart remembered how this landowner friend, Captain Freddie Wentworth, RN, mighty Lord of the Manor of Aldeburgh, had been defeated in a lengthy legal battle by a not-so-simple boat-owner fisherman, a famous coxswain of the Thorpeness 'Blue Lifeboat'. William Alexander had had his collection of huts, sheds, fishing-boats and tackle by the side of the estuary and reared his family there for well over twenty years 'without let or hindrance'. Then, in the late 1880's he had suddenly claimed the land as 'Squatter's Rights' from the Lord of the Manor. After a long court case followed avidly by all, he won - to the jubilation of his friends. Stuart liked that. It showed the

Sizewell Hall, July 1914 - egg and spoon race at a Primrose League Fete

sand-dunes and the broad tidal fen known as Thorpe mere. Away to the west, this mere was fed by the little River Hundred from Aldringham which followed its meandering course until it was caught up in the surge of salt water sweeping in and out with the tide from the estuary just south of his land. Until recently the water also swept on southwards into the silted-up Thorpe Haven, reaching

buccaneering spirit was not dead. Besides, William Alexander and his son Alfred were his friends who used to accompany him and his younger brother, Menteith, as boys when wildfowling. The wily old man then sold the valuable site and the prestigious Haven House was built, while he proudly moved to a 'real house' in Thorpe across the heath from the Crown Inn (now the Dolphin). This old cottage immediately became known as 'Alexander's House' (later, now enlarged, as 'Alexander House').

The two young Ogilvie brothers had had so many adventures on the mere and fens in their flat-bottomed duck punt. Stuart recalled how they became seafaring invaders - Frisians who settled in Fris-ton, and the

In olden times, Stuart reflected, Thorpe Haven (sometimes called Thorpe Hithe, South Haven, Almouth or Portus de Almouth) had been a vital landmark to the many small trading ships which had plied their way up and down the coast, also for traders coming across the sea from France or Holland, some stopping on their way to

Alexander House in 1977

chieftain leader Knod who built his hall nearby at Knodishall and brought over his family and livestock in flat-bottomed barges; then, the Jutes, Saxons, and ferocious Vikings. They were not all bad, though, they had been told - as the name Aldringham proved. This in Anglo-Saxon 'Allrinc's Ham', meant 'Foreign but Honourable Warrior's Hamlet', (as from Ipswich Archives: "Suffolk Chronicles (1950) Suffolk Names").

It was here, by the little church, where their mother, Margaret Ogilvie, built her Almshouses in 1890, that quantities of Saxon pottery and artefacts were found. The young explorers had discovered them all, paddling their sharp-bowed craft through the winding waterways and reeds. They even ventured south, too, into foreign Wentworth waters beyond the estuary - inhabited by smugglers and wild tribes.

London. Tradesmen of various kinds had therefore set up business alongside the estuary and also the banks in Aldeburgh, as shown on old maps (one of which (of Eliz.1) hangs in the Moot Hall today). These became thriving settlements, even building sizeable boats.

Between 1565 and 1568, Thorpe and Aldeburgh had the largest number of fishing boats in Suffolk, (as recorded by the "Victoria County of Suffolk"), and the County of Suffolk was providing one seventh of the nation's shipping. Thorpe Haven was already silting up, however, and after 1576 the heavier boats with deeper keels sailed to or were made at the new quay at Slaughtinge or Slaughden, (from the Anglo-Saxon 'Slog-dene', a muddy place - Ipswich Archives).

Stuart sadly regretted the decline of Thorpe from a bustling trading port to a refuge and safe harbour only. Inevitably, the population had then drifted away. The hamlet of Torp or Thorpe was old when it was mentioned in Domesday Book in 1086. Thorpe Ness, the promontory to the north of the village, used to be much larger and is recorded on all subsequent maps - as was the now crumbling remains of St Mary's Chapel. Like nearly all other cliff-top churches, it had served also as a landmark and warning to

with sluggish water moving in a random network of little channels scattered in marsh reeds. The mouth of the estuary was choked up again, as it had not been cleared for some time. Little tide, therefore, came in. The River Hundred itself had dwindled as other landowners higher up the stream had also drained their land. This meant that it did not have the flow to carry away the silt and the

An early view of old Thorpe opposite the Meare

sailors. Each of these churches carried a lantern on its spire or tower or, if lacking these, on a pole on its roof. On old navigation maps he had seen, Stuart remembered, St Mary's was depicted as a small spire. He wondered who tended it. The last reference to the little chapel being used (recorded in the Norfolk & Norwich Records Office) seemed to have been in 1608 when a marriage took place in it despite it being reported that "the church of Thorpe is ruinous and hath been for a whole year". By then the Dissolution of the Monasteries and Henry VIII's henchmen had done their worst, their mother priory at Snape was demolished and many churches closed.

Now as Stuart scanned the flat, treeless village, it had a forsaken, desolate air. All was changed since the Wentworths had drained their haven. Thorpe mere was boggy,

'blue-slipper clay' or 'ewe' which it brought down, so both the river and the mere were silting up.

As if to contradict this, there were times after prolonged rain when the little River Hundred was in spate, so that if the estuary were barred with shingle the mere flooded over into the rough road and also the Wentworths' newly drained pasture land. This had happened dramatically in 1904, when Stuart's mother and Captain Freddie had shared the cost of clearing the sand and shingle barring the outlet to the sea. Twenty-four men were employed to clear the hundred and seventy-five yards to a depth of 5 ft. Three days hard work, in which hundreds of tons of shingle were removed, brought about the desired effect. The fishermen, alerted by flocks of screaming seagulls, realised that fish had been trapped and were being carried along the channel to the sea. They therefore sought by means of nets to intercept them. This revealed literally tons of eels. One fisherman with two men to help him filled two large punts to capacity between seven at night and four in the morning. Many eels were five or six pounders, and 2,240 lbs were despatched to London. "Fishermen took over £200 that night," it was reported in the East Anglian Daily Times, who called it 'The Great Harvest of Eels'.

Stuart liked to see the mere covered in water, with just a few little reedy islands. He also wished he could resurrect the little chapel which had meant so much to people of long ago, but now there was no congregation, no real village. People had moved away. White's Gazetteer had described Thorpe as having only '142 souls': Stuart wondered if it now had as many. Kelly's Directory reminded people that the village had had its days of excitement: invasion, seafaring adventures, piracy, smuggling. Now the village seemed sleeping. Dormant. An idea was crystallising in Stuart's mind. It was crazy. Quite mad! But suddenly he felt more excited than when he had a wonderful idea for a new play. Somehow, he would put life back into the little hamlet. He would recreate Thorpe. He would build houses, clubs, the chapel - pump

breath back into its heart - and he would make the heart not the beach but a great lake, "the other dimension": the mere.

No-one could say that Stuart Ogilvie, in spite of his visionary fervour, was not a realist. To create a village he had to have inhabitants. The only way to get these quickly was, he realised, to make his village - at least at first - a seaside holiday village. This, too, would make it viable. Soon it should pay for itself. But his new Thorpe would be different, quite unlike any other seaside development (which he hated). He would have no vulgar piers and pierrots or side-shows. No smart promenade flanked by swanky hotels and the everlasting straggle of dreary boarding-houses which proliferated everywhere. Nor would he try to compete with Brighton or Aldeburgh. This would always be a village. A beautiful village for those who appreciated Beauty. A family place for relaxation, combined with health-giving sports for those who wanted them. There must be a need for such a holiday village. For families like his own, cultured but not stuffy and boring - where children could run free, have adventures, make voyages of discovery - and the parents could relax in peace.

For his village, Stuart decided he would turn back from the dull, lifeless, modern

Man with dancing bear in front of the Meare in the 1890s

architecture and revive the spirit and feeling of his beloved Tudor Age. The age of 'Merrie England', using wooden cladding and beams, curved roads and quaint corners. The old and the new would blend harmoniously. Like a picture or well-designed stage set, it would be a work of art - and, as such, it would have to be the creation of one single, imaginative brain.

He hurried home and sketched it all, beginning with the roads, round the old tracks and natural formation of the land. He planned for every house (no two to be exactly alike), a club (the social centre), a water-tower with a windmill (because it would be so picturesque), a church, a shop, a boat-house, and even a splendid hotel with shops underneath - as he had seen in Chester. He knew this would have to come later, as also would Almshouses, a Workmen's Club, and other amenities. Sporting facilities were planned, to included tennis, croquet, a golf-course, and, of course the mere - which he decided he would spell 'Meare' as on Elizabethan maps. This will be "beautiful beyond comparison" he averred "and a children's paradise and adults' joy".

Only when he had laid out his plans for the whole village, including sketches, did Stuart consult his architect friend, W. G. Wilson (who had worked with him when he enlarged Sizewell Hall), and also a young architect from Southsea who already visited Thorpe, Forbes Glennie, LRIBA. They were both enthusiastic about the idea of working on this unusual and long-term project. Stuart made it clear that *he* was to be the overall Designer - or Production Manager - of the village. He would hand over his sketches and working plans, and seek their criticisms - but the credit would go to them as architects. They were the professionals: they did all the work. Certainly neither of them had thought of designing anything like his strange buildings: not even made of bricks, but of concrete and timber. In fact, they doubted the wisdom or possibility of some of his plans.

There were, however, some snags (Stuart explained) that he had to get over before he could begin. One was that he did not actually own the mere. If Lord Rendlesham would sell it to him, he would first have to persuade Captain Wentworth to allow him to dam up Thorpe mere with sluice gates from the River Hundred entrance and make an exit sluice gate in their common boundary bank, with a dyke to carry both the River Hundred and Thorpe mere surplus water to join the Wentworth sluice outlet, to be pumped into the sea with the surplus water from Captain Wentworth's land.

Fortunately, consent was cordially given - helped, no doubt, by old friendships and perhaps by the fact that Stuart's younger son, Sholto, had recently married the young and beautiful Gladys Rooke, whose mother was a Thellusson, the late Lord Rendlesham's granddaughter, and whose late grandmother was a Wentworth. The families were already on good terms in Alexander Ogilvie's day.

The last hurdle Stuart had to tackle was to obtain permission from the Lord of the Manor to buy the whole of Thorpe, freehold. At the time he owned certain buildings and some land, but only had a lease on the rest. Furthermore, of recent years all applications for building sites had been refused, due "possibly to the Tin Tabernacle school of bungalow architecture which had grown up upon the benthills," Stuart wrote later. However, once Lord Huntingfield had seen the plans and strict undertakings had been agreed, he willingly sold Stuart the 290 odd acres which comprised the site of the new Thorpe. This, Stuart decided to rename Thorpeness in order to distinguish it from other Thorpes in the country.

With legal obstacles now removed and matters tied up, Stuart, fired with visionary enthusiasm, could not wait to get started. At last he could tell Graeme Kemp about his exciting Thorpeness plan, and that they would begin with the 'heart' of his 'dream' - the Meare.

Chapter Two

Creation Begins

GRAEME Kemp remembered: "It was on a damp November day in 1910. Mr Stuart and I were standing looking over the mere which was again somewhat flooded and looking particularly dismal and desolate."

It was a feverishly busy time but very exhilarating, Graeme recalled. First, the banks and sluice gates at the mouth of the little River Hundred had to be made and the water diverted to a dyke round the southern

The mouth of the Meare, c.1890

"Graeme, I think it would be a good idea to turn this into a lake," Stuart said. "I have some sketches here." He shuffled through them. "Will you get out some plans for me? You are going to be my Master of Works in creating a model holiday village."

Work began immediately, and Graeme and "Happy" Knights surveyed the shape chosen and the acreage - sixty-two acres of water. Meanwhile, Stuart formed a development company, Seaside Bungalows Ltd., with a capital of £5,000, which he registered for £5 in the Isle of Man for tax purposes.

boundary to Captain Wentworth's wind pump. They borrowed a hand-operated pile-driver from the Minsmere Level Commissioners and put in the two sluice gates. Fortunately, they had on the estate an expert in sluice gates and dam building, also in sea defences and well sinking, Ted Friend, from the old Mill House, Westleton. This versatile craftsman had already sunk a well for old Mrs Margaret Ogilvie at "Ted's Barn", Sizewell, and a new deeper well for Stuart at Sizewell Hall. At a glance he knew the exact quantity and type of material required for each job. The piles for the sluice were from Brown's of Ipswich, and were of Russian larch, 20 ft long, sharply pointed, and with iron-shod tops. One was driven in on the slope with another beside it used for the dam. The 9 ft by 9 ft walls were tongue and grooved. The banks were built in the old tried medieval way of crossed staves, heather and willows, mud and pummelled with clay.

"I don't like the look of that", Stuart had remarked dolefully to Graeme, to which the latter had replied "Fools and bairns should ne'er see unfinished work." As Graeme said, "You couldn't make a remark like that to most masters but he always took it well.."

To speed up the task of digging out the lake, Stuart had the brilliant idea of giving work to some of London's unemployed. He

The Meare before 1914

The south sluice gates were then opened and the mere allowed to drain. It took three weeks. Muddy banks were then built up and strengthened.

Stuart, surveying the vast muddy waste, for once was almost daunted by the task. The hard causeway made by his father when building the Leiston-Aldeburgh railway line constructed by Brassey & Ogilvie, now stood out clearly. It ran from the eastern shore (where the boating pay kiosk is today) in a strip approximately 15 feet wide, down to the Three Arches sheep-wash bridge in the west. It was used to carry stones on a light railway pulled by a horse, for ballast when laying the lines. Apart from this, the ground was an uneven morass of pools, humps of islands, and channels.

arranged for about fifty to be sent down by train and had them put up at 'The Shellpits' (the erstwhile Children's Convalescent Home on Aldringham Common) and catered for. However, the weather was bitter; the men sent were unfit and unused to 'navvy' work. They begged to be allowed to go home. They liked the food but they were utterly miserable - and useless. At the end of the week they were paid and put on a train back to London.

After this, Stuart decided to rely on local labour. Together with some of his own men, they engaged sixteen fishermen, who with their high fishermen's boots and oilies thought nothing of floundering in the mud in all weathers. These men changed with others when they took time off for fishing. Each morning Stuart would be seen on his roan horse, Dick, riding at a furious pace across the common to join them. He would plunge into the bog and wade around directing where the next island was to be made or the channel cleared, often shovelling away himself and testing the depth. It was vital that the 'blue-slipper clay' or 'ewe' was not pierced. The great fear being that the water would then disappear into the sandy sub-soil like bath water down the plug-hole. Not more than two feet of mud was to be cleared, therefore, which meant when filled the Meare would not be deeper anywhere than two feet six inches. The sludge was then dragged away on skids or on a temporary light rail track, and piled up and pummelled into islands with heather and whin to make up the banks. The enthusiasm was catching and the work progressed at amazing speed.

Meanwhile, on the edge of the morass, the boat-house was already being built by Smythe of Leiston - for the cost of £419.8s.7d. It was an attractive design, made out of wood, and Stuart could not resist making the clock tower also like a dovecote. Here again, he would install white fantails, as at Sizewell. The first four houses in The Haven were under construction by Ward of Aldringham. William Reade of Aldeburgh had the contract for the rest of The Haven and The Whinlands (as Stuart had named the continuation of the road down to "The Crown") with prices varying from £298 to £384 each. Although running water was being laid on, none of these houses (which were built for summer use only) had amenities beyond open fires, an "Ideal" stove for heating the water and an earth closet outside the back door (to be followed later by a w.c.) This would be emptied every night by a "night-soil" man. Oil lamps were provided and all houses were going to be fully furnished to a high standard and complete with crockery and silver (hotel type plate) but not linen - unless specifically asked for, when it could be hired. These basic amenities were the norm in country villages at the time.

The interesting thing about these houses was the way they were built. Remembering his father's method when constructing various docks, the foundations and lower half of the buildings were to be made of concrete with Portland Cement. The walls were built between shutters in stages, allowing the first stage to dry and harden before pouring in the second. The upper halves were mostly of wood and plaster with mock Tudor beams set in. It was a method both quick and relatively cheap.

At the same time Seaside Bungalows Ltd. was building an Assembly Room, or Club House with a bar, where residents could meet, dance and play cards, tennis or croquet. It would be the social centre for the village and concerts or dramatics could also take place on the stage there. In fact, it would be very similar to an Officer's Club in India and run by a social secretary.

To build up a viable and happy community, Stuart knew that it was vital to provide a centre which, if they wished, people could (with suitable introductions or credentials) join to meet other people of like interests. There would be nothing in Thorpeness to encourage or please those seeking the fun of the "penny peep-show", minstrels on the pier, or the thrill of the swings, switchbacks and roundabouts.

During this period of feverish activity, Graeme Kemp had his men doing all the back-up work needed. On the Meare, already thousands of willows, sallows and alders were being planted, taken from cuttings from the Sizewell and Minsmere marshes. Stuart supervised the lay-out, so that there was variety. The larger islands would also carry oaks, ilex and a conifer or poplar here and there. The banks, too, were surrounded in greenery, shrubs, yellow flags, and bulrushes. A well was being sunk by Ted Friend for a somewhat primitive Mediterranean-looking wind pump, with five canvas sails, to supply water to the Club. This was to start as just one building, sitting on a sand dune, to be called "The Kursaal". Another new mill on the Uplands Common north of the Meare would supply water for the village. Old Thorpe already had a number of wells including one at "The Crown" with a public pump. It was quite common for those less fortunate to rely solely on their rainwater tank, in which case the water was "filtered" through a cloth to "get the wigglies out". The better off had a special stone water-jar with a lid. This was filled with white "honey-combed" material - stones or ceramic - which filtered the water, and it came out cool from the tap below. Those with "bucket" wells often used these jars for convenience and purity, too. Graeme Kemp's household had one of these when he was young.

Another of Graeme's tasks was making up the main curving road through the village, which was no more than a sandy lane. Road works up to date had been the responsibility of one man, Tommy Brame, who, because of his limited mental capacity, was given the job of going round with a spade and barrow, filling up pot-holes, under the supervision of Ben Harling who kept the shop (now enlarged as "Sea View") on the sandy Benthills. Beside this was a small wooden shop where "Stab-Rag" Dale, the tailor, sat cross-legged in his window and would make or mend just about anything. Graeme was to

make a proper road here, too, for the visitors' carriages or motor cars, when they came.

The method used was the well-tried one, common in this part of the world. This consisted of :

- Digging out 1 ft deep of the road and levelling;
- Spreading whin bushes (gorse) in layers;
- Piling in brick rubble and rubbish from houses;
- Covering with clay (from pits at Beacon Hill, behind Beacon Hill Lane, which strangely had clay at the near end and sharp sand at the other);
- Scattering a good layer of pebbles off the beach (no longer to be fetched by hand but to be pulled up in buckets on a pulley and overhead cable, originally set up by the Ogilvie children for fun rides and now moved to Ted's Barn). From thence, the pebbles were to be transported in the small trucks on the light railway (which had originally been used across the Meare) and drawn by horse to a place opposite the Crown, whence they were taken out and spread over the road with rubble;
- After which, this was rolled with a heavy horse roller.
- In dusty weather it was to be sprayed with a weak tar solution by a horse-drawn sprinkler. This would last all the summer.

Seaview at the turn of the century, showing Ben Harling's shop on the left and Stab-Rag's shop on the right

Stuart came from an inventive family. His father, Alexander, had been one of the first to use Portland Cement in dock building, and to advocate the "steam-shovel", and was the first in this country to use a steam-crane for removing the spoil when he built the twelve-mile Metropolitan Mid-Level Sewer beneath the heart of London. It was not surprising, therefore, that Stuart also encouraged his children (much aided by their engineering-minded cousins) in their various adventurous experiments: hence the construction of a high tower on the bank at Cliff House and the

level crossing at Leiston and the Brick Dock Works at Aldeburgh. Graeme also made use of the flints and ancient masonry lying around the ruined remains of St Mary's Chapel in Chapel Field (today, behind the Almshouses and Pilgrim's Way).

Stuart had already decided that his new church would revive the name of St Mary, but would stand on the "windy hill" looking out to sea, just north of Chapel House (in what is now Church Road). The original chapel, a brick building, was built in the early 18th century and appears on the earliest

William Kemp in his sulky

detailed maps, coming into the ownership of the Ogilvies in 1873. It was run by Dissenters and frowned on by "the Church". Joe Wilson preached there in the 1890's and was renowned for his fierce addresses and his spirited playing of the fiddle for the singing. Women's meetings also took place in this Chapel, and old Mrs Margaret Ogilvie had a small harmonium installed for them. Then, during a great storm, a gale blew the thatched roof off and caused much damage, leaving the building derelict. After this, the locals attended the Fishermens' Bethel - the "Tin Tabernacle" on the land opposite the Meare. After the formation of Seaside Bungalows Ltd. Stuart purchased Chapel House from Sizewell Estates and had it repaired and tiled. As there was no further use for it as a chapel, Graeme said, it became a house which was then let on lease.

bucket-run to the beach, on the lines of a coastguards' breeches-buoy. (This had gone furiously fast and well until one day his young niece, Kathleen, became suspended about 30 ft up for over half an hour when the pulley became entangled with the return rope for pulling the empty bucket back, and Helen, his wife, decreed that the experiment was "proved" and should be discontinued!) It was now proving invaluable in its new role of raising pebbles up the cliff.

Thorpeness was well placed for brickyards and rubble. Old William Kemp, the builder, (Graeme's grandfather) got most of his bricks from the Brick Kiln just north of his house, Hawsell's Farm, in Leiston. Then there was Carr's Pit and Brickfield, just north of the

Stuart thought long about his new church, which he wished to build in memory of his mother and for all that she had stood for in her attitude to "true" religion - a progressive revelation which embraced all sects. First,

Aftermath of the storm of October 1911 - "Shorecote" already gone, "Seadune" teetering on the brink

however, he knew he had to build more houses.

Building was going on at speed, punctuated by a few local diversions, such as the Thorpeness Marine Regatta. This was a high day and holiday for all, instigated in 1911, which drew people to the beach from the neighbouring towns and villages.

Then came the disastrous autumn storm in October 1911. As well as producing the highest tide and deepest scourings in memory, this demolished huts and bungalows on the beach, and "Shorecote" toppled dangerously half over the eroded cliff and had to be moved to a safer site in what is now North End Avenue. The storm also brought great excitement to the village and in particular to Alfred Alexander and his friends. As the sea raged over the "pentlands" that night, eroding and scouring away the topsoil of centuries, it exposed what all "polterers" or "gallooners" dreamed of finding. (This 16th century Dutch phrase for searchers for treasures from ships - from "Polteren voor een Galjoen" - was still in use

at this time). Alfred had been a "polterer" all his life and was always out at first daylight after a storm. He had been lucky in the past - gold and silver pieces of the Edwards, Elizabeth and Charles 1, and, more frequently, articles of cargo or contraband thrown or washed overboard. This time the find was the greatest he and his friends had ever found. Exposed by the scour in a hollow lay a veritable treasure - 110 pieces of various coins, including Roman ones.

News of the treasure caused such a stir - the papers were full of it - that an inquest was held at the Moot Hall with "an impressive body of adjudicators, the County Coroner, three assessors, and a jury of thirteen local residents, to decide whether or not the Crown could claim the right of Treasure Trove." The main question was whether or not the goods had been found below or above an ordinary high tide. If below, the Crown could legally claim Treasure Trove. Most of the articles and coins belonged to the period 1216 to 1685, and as a number of wells had been revealed close to where the coins had been found, it was deduced that this area had been inhabited at that time. It was the officials who finally turned the scales in favour of the finders, and the Coroner declared in the ancient formula - "that various persons had deposited in land at Thorpe gold and silver, owners not known, and the coins were not the property of our Lord the King."

The finders' prize, however, was not their own yet because the Receiver of Wrecks (who had taken charge of the find until the Inquest) did not find it convenient to return it. It was only after the persistent Alfred Alexander and his friends had the matter raised in Parliament that eventually the "finders" became "keepers".

Stuart, with his sense of drama, naturally followed the cause of his old friend avidly. His boyish love of adventure stories, pirates and hidden treasure had not left him. This, too, gave him a further inspired idea: could he incorporate on the scenic Meare a children's adventure treasure hunt?

It was not enough just to make it an exciting but safe watery region of hidden rivers and mysterious islands but - a sudden inspiration struck him - he would scatter them with little play-houses and fantasies taken from well-known children's books: "The Pirates' Lair", "The Smugglers' Cave", "Peter Pan's Property", "Wendy's House", "The Magic Pavilion", "Crusoe's Island" ... He sketched an "Ancient Chart" with an Armada Galleon in "The Spanish Main", a crocodile, a dragon ... He loved it. He could have spent all day on it.

He was already writing his first publicity brochure "Seaside Bungalows" on his new-style holiday village (extolling the fact that private enterprise was building it and running it, to combat the evil of bureaucratic socialism), that would be of special appeal to cultured families with young children. Now he would include this unique feature in it.

He would ask his friend J. M. Barrie if he could use his Peter Pan (copyright) names,

Picnic at The Kursaal (now the Country Club) for workmen's families, 1912

and then name the lakeside bay path after him: "Barrie's Walk". Barrie would like that!

In the spring of 1912, the main building of "The Kursaal", or assembly rooms and club house, was finished. A picnic was given to the men who had worked on it, and their families and children invited. The Boathouse was also completed, and, as much of the Meare was navigable, Graeme was sent all round the country to pick up small (second-hand) dinghies, rowing and sailing boats, canoes, punts, and anything he thought suitable. He started with three or four dozen, each priced from £3 up (most of which are still in use today). The Thorpeness Kursaal Club was to be officially opened on Saturday, May 25th 1912. Stuart was determined this should go well so as to set the standard for the club's future. His friend, the London solicitor Sir William Bull, MP, agreed to come and open it, and invitations were sent out. Stuart pored over his speech outlining his purpose and plans, with emphasis on family holidays, sport and "the children's paradise" - the Meare in the making. Days went by and few people answered. He became increasingly alarmed. Stage fright he was used to ... the author's dread of an empty auditorium. Suppose no-one came? Suppose no-one liked the idea? Suppose it was all a disaster? To see this tall, powerful man striding confidently around the village, no-one could have imagined that success was doubted. One unlikely person, however, had reason to know: Miss Nell Webster, Schoolmistress of Aldringham School, the eldest daughter of the saddler and shoemaker at Elm Tree Farm.

In 1977, when she was a sprightly ninety-one (and still treasurer of Aldringham Church) she loved to recount stories of the old days. She remembered how old Mrs

The opening of The Kursaal (now the Country Club) in 1912 - G. Stuart Ogilvie on lower step to left, beside Sir William Bull. Helen Ogilvie on top row of steps, on right, with arm on rail

Ogilvie would drive up in her phaeton to see Nell's father about her saddlery: her private horses always had to have silver trappings, which she brought to him. Mrs Ogilvie had a habit, too, of losing her keys for her cupboards or caskets, and would send for Mr Webster to come round with his bag of tools to open them for her. She always took a great interest in people, especially children, and was very kind.

Nell also remembered Stuart well: "Of course I knew Mr Stuart!" she said. "I remember him coming to me before the opening of this club - the Kursaal, they called it. He was so afraid there would hardly be anyone there that he asked me if I could bring all the children along. I said of course I would. Then suddenly at the last minute all the County accepted and he feared he wouldn't have room for them all, so he came to me and said "I hate to have to ask you and it's not a nice thing to do but I will go down on my knees to you and be eternally grateful to you if you can - " (he was a bit of an actor, wasn't he?) - so I said "Well, what is it, then?" and he said "*Could* you go round to all those

children and tell them I'm sorry there will be no room for them after all - and explain why? I hate to disappoint them, so make it good to them." So I said "Why, yes, I'll go round" and I remember he went down on his knee and took my hand and said "Thank you, dear lady, thank you!" She chuckled. "And I remember thinking to myself "That's a cold step to kneel on!"

Fortunately, all went well for the official opening. The club already had a sizeable and distinguished membership of local and London people, as Stuart had included boating on the half-made Meare in the membership. When fully finished, the Meare was to be officially opened by Lord Huntingfield. It would then also be open to the public. This was scheduled for June 1913.

Visitors were already taking the new houses as they were built, as summer or weekend homes. As another amenity to the village, Stuart opened "The Mart" (on the present site of the Sports and Social Club) and encouraged traders to form a market in the large wooden building he put up. This was under the able management of

Gunthorpe's of Leiston, selling a wide range of goods: groceries, butcher's meat, vegetables, fish, oil, etc., pending the building of permanent shops.

Meantime, house-building continued. The New Mill was erected. This was a large tank on an iron frame, with an American windmill, and was for the time being a very ugly structure. Roads, cesspits and other necessities were appearing at a great rate. Croquet and tennis were already in full swing at the Kursaal, and dancing and concerts had become regular features All through the winter, work pressed forward on all fronts. There were teams of men on the Meare, the roads, and concrete-making (which they now were making into large slab bricks). The architects' department was busy; and, most important, men were engaged in tree-planting and laying out the gardens (which had to be finished with each completed house).

Stuart was delighted. Everything was going as planned, and he personally oversaw every detail, down to the colour of the wallflowers and the type and placing of each rose.

He was pleased, too, that he had just negotiated with the Great Eastern Railway to provide a Halt at Thorpe now it was a growing holiday resort - to be called Thorpeness Halt. All trains on the spur line from Aldeburgh or Saxmundham/Leiston would stop there. It would open in July of 1914. Stuart had already formed a company, with Graeme Kemp as Chairman, called Thorpeness Vitesse Ltd., to buy cars (and spare parts) to transport their visitors to and from Leiston station, and also to put on outings to local places of interest. One novel idea of Stuart's was to buy an old double-decker London horse-bus and tow it behind his very large old daimler to be used as a station bus. He replaced the upper structure and seats of the car body with that of another old horsedrawn bus. The upper structure, however, proved too heavy for the car engine and was replaced with a canopy. The discarded top was then adapted and put on what was grandly called "The Stage Barge"

Thorpeness Halt

Daimler pulling a London horse bus, 1913

or "The Royal George" - an Eventrude motor launch - to take people on a tour of the Meare. However, it had to be abandoned after the second season due to its weight, as the propellers got caught in the weeds which had grown up. There was also a smaller motor launch, "The Gee-Whizz", which had to be withdrawn after a season, due to endless trouble.

Nothing was wasted in Thorpeness, and the old bus top, complete with its red plush facing seats, was then again removed and converted into "The House of the Seven Dwarfs" on one of the islands. The Flying Dragon that had been added to its roof was transferred to the roof of "The Magic Pavilion" - originally a beach hut called "Rusticana".

The early 20th century was not a "throw-away" age and at Thorpeness, where every penny was needed for its rapid expansion, every labour-saving device or innovation was used - or re-used - if it would save money. At that time, fashionable seaside resorts had bathing-machines for hire on the beach. These were expensive, and needed attendants

The State Barge "The Royal George", 1912

23

and a horse to haul them up and down according to the tide. Stuart, therefore, proudly made a feature of Thorpeness not needing them. It was a family resort for gentlefolk, not surrounded by a busy town. With its unique privately-owned beach, any undesirable persons would be sent off. In Thorpeness, families could wander down to the beach in their bathrobes. In fact, it was the custom. For those, however, who did prefer a changing hut, the Kursaal Club provided "Dhoolie Bathing Cabins" (invented and constructed on the estate) which were carried down for them. These

Anything less than perfection would not do. Suppose there was some ghastly fiasco in the kitchen? Had he struck the right note with his speech? He went over it again. As his friend Henry Irving used to say - "it's the timing that counts - mark the pauses - the easy gesture .." Stuart need not have worried. Everything went faultlessly. The County all turned up. Both local and London press were there in numbers, with cameras clicking. The reports were ecstatic.

Among others, next day the Leiston Observer gave the event full-page coverage, capturing the spirit of the proceedings

Dhoolie bathing cabin, 1912 (Mrs. William Kemp inside!)

were, in fact, rarely used (there were only two), but Stuart found "The Dhoolie" was excellent publicity value and was pictured widely in the local and London press. The East Anglian Daily Times reported that the first year's operation of the Kursaal and Boating Club was a resounding success, with over a hundred members.

At last dawned the day of the Meare's official opening: Wednesday, June 11th 1913. As usual before an "opening night" Stuart was nervous. Would the people come? Would the weather hold fine? Would the luncheon he was putting on in the Club be edible?

admirably. It re-stated the joys and safety of the Children's Paradise, also what a pleasure it was to see the wildlife being drawn to the Meare by all its new plantings - exceeding all that had been there when it was used only by wildfowlers. The article extolled the development so far and looked forward to the arrival of the railway to bring more visitors to enjoy the region. A description of the excellent luncheon followed, and a list of all the local celebrities present.

"The Great Eastern Railway had invited a large party of journalists and other gentlemen to visit the new Suffolk resort," the Leiston

Observer continued. "These travelled from Liverpool Street to Leiston, where they were met by the Vitesse Motor Train and other motor cars closely following each other, bringing out many sightseers from their houses along the route. "Before the opening" it said, "Lord Huntingfield made an inspection of the Boy Scouts of Leiston and Aldeburgh, and music was supplied by the Band of the Leiston Company of the 4th Battalion Suffolks. Mr G. Stuart Ogilvie in opening the proceedings welcomed all those present and reminded them that it was barely a year ago that many of them were here at the opening of the Thorpeness Kursaal, an event which he liked to describe as the birth of Thorpeness as they had taken the unusual decision and daring step of building a commodious club-house, in spacious pleasure grounds, with two double 'En tout cas' hard courts before a single bungalow was built. "This was just to show what we were going to do," he said. "We are now assembled together to witness what I may term the christening of this baby village of Thorpeness." He could not help but feel a little proud of this large assemblage of important people who had come from far and near to attend this christening "... and profound thanks to you, my lord, for presiding at this ceremony today." He also gave warm thanks to Captain Vernon Wentworth for co-operating in the management of the water to enable the Meare to be constructed. He gave, too, a special welcome to the Mayor of Aldeburgh, "as" he said "his presence must put an end to the idle and senseless idea that our baby Thorpeness may, in some mysterious way, compete with or injure her big sister Aldeburgh ... Thorpeness will never attempt to rival Aldeburgh", he said "or, I fear, rise to the dignity of a Mayor and Corporation". He also suggested that the Meare would prove as great an asset and source of pleasure for adults and children from Aldeburgh as it was to those of Thorpeness, adding that they would not, however, get the full benefit of the thousands of pounds expended by Seaside Bungalows until the much looked for completion of the carriage road from Aldeburgh to Thorpeness. This contentious point brought loud cries of "Hear, Hear!" Ever since the Jubilee Bridge was built in 1897 to replace the rickety 'Rattlebone' footbridge by the ford, with its single handrail, the promised road was still awaited. The rough sandy track from the bridge which ran behind the few houses on the benthills was totally unsuitable for present traffic.

Mr Ogilvie then pointed out, "with certain pride" (the Observer said) "how hard everyone had worked and how in little over a year the Company had - in addition to building and equipping the Kursaal and the Boat-house, extending the Meare, building more roads and building or reconstructing thirty more bungalows - sunk a deep well provided with a powerful American windmill, and laid the necessary mains connection to bring the water to the club-house and every bungalow on the estate - and the water analysed was found to be of the highest purity. Further, each bungalow will be supplied through a shilling-in-the-slot meter, with acetylene gas (at about half the price of coal gas in any neighbouring town). Thorpeness will then have the distinction of becoming the very first township in Great Britain to be lighted throughout by acetylene gas. So, you see, our baby promises to be as precocious as she is beautiful!" he said, to laughter and applause.

"One further word about the economics of Thorpeness," he added. "A peculiar and particular popular feature of the Company's leases is that they are offered at a rent which covers all outgoings, including rates, taxes and even the water rate. The Company also undertakes to maintain the little bijoux gardens, supplying the necessary seeds and flowers, cutting the lawns, etc., for a very low sum per annum, if desired. Moreover, if any bungalow is damaged by the sea, the

Thompson, Mayor of Aldeburgh, who announced that the project of having a road between Aldeburgh and Thorpeness was receiving consideration.

Everyone cheered. The ceremony was over. The band, now in punts, struck up with a cheerful air over the water. The Scouts and populace rushed for boats, and, packed to the gunnels, proceeded with much merriment and varying skill on their hazardous journey of exploration. The dignitaries moved back to the Kursaal for afternoon tea."

The great event had gone off well, Stuart thought. Everyone was happy. Thorpeness should now - if the journalists did their stuff - be on the map. He ended the day "Quite satisfied" - which meant that he was more than delighted.

As the summer proceeded the Meare was a great attraction. All the bungalows (as these two-storeyed houses were still called, following the fashion in India) were snapped up as soon as they were ready. Stuart was elated that the visitors' reactions were as he had foreseen. The visitors remarked on, and loved, the colourful gardens, constructed and planted as each house was built. They found the personal service (including daily maids and domestic staff where needed) was exceptional.

Nothing was too much trouble, and everyone felt part of the development. At the end of the season, Stuart was more than satisfied. He had worked hard with his publicity and kept the press well posted, while journalists for the glossy magazines came to take photographs of 'notables' and

lease of that bungalow ipso facto ceases. The inclusive Thorpeness rents are therefore, the Company claims, some fifteen to twenty per cent below those of any other town of similar conveniences in Britain."

He ended by saying he hoped that today they were "assisting in the inauguration of what will, in a few brief years, have grown into one of the beauty spots in Suffolk and afford golden hours of happy, healthy recreation now and long after we and the words we speak today pass into the limbo of forgotten things."

The Observer continued "After the loud and prolonged applause died down, Lord Huntingfield rose, and in the course of a racy speech said that he hoped to find something in the paper that day about Home Rule. He could not see it anywhere, but instead saw his name in large letters as about to open the Meare. He gave praise for the development and all that had been achieved and what it stood for ... and had the greatest pleasure possible in opening the Meare.

Cordial thanks were given to him, proposed by Sir Frederick Adair, the first President of the Kursaal & Meare Boating Club, and similar compliments were paid to Mr G. Stuart Ogilvie on the motion of Mr report on new developments or events - such as a performance by the Carl Rosa Opera Company (conveniently, his brother Menteith's daughter, Marjorie, sang in this). The Great Eastern Railway, too, was kept well supplied with copies of his illustrated "Guide to Thorpeness" for their bookstalls and prestigious hotels.

Stuart was determined that Thorpeness was going to be run on proper business lines. He was not, in any case, the fabulously wealthy man that people thought he was. To

Through the winter of 1913, work continued on all fronts, with weekly meetings to report progress. In March 1914, as work increased and grew more involved, Stuart formed the new Thorpeness Advisory Committee to assist in the management of Seaside Bungalows Ltd. A financial statement had to be produced each week showing the balance at the Bank, the takings each week (if any) of each department, and the once-fortnightly capital outlay (if any) and how it was apportioned.

Crowds watch the pillow fight at Thorpeness Regatta, 1913

undertake in a matter of a few years the huge project of erecting a whole village - which had no infrastructure and little vegetation - he knew was going to mean investing a vast amount of capital and would necessitate careful economy. Needless to say, he had eager offers to "go in with him" to form partnerships or employ property developers. Such suggestions were anathema to him. "I am not a common property developer" he often declared, and would add: "If I were, I would simply cover the ground with hideous monstrosities such as we see all too frequently elsewhere - and doubtless make a fortune in so doing." He would also insist that he was an artist, creating an ideal village in a setting of surpassing beauty, for those who appreciate peace and the finer things of life. "An Art Village," he would affirm "can only be the work of one single mind - the Artist."

The duties and responsibilities of each member were clearly defined, covering every aspect and detail of the enterprise from buildings to catering and games, so nothing was overlooked and all ran smoothly and was reported on regularly.

By the spring of 1914, all available houses were fully booked for the season, and all various works going according to plan. The Company was delighted and full of enthusiasm. The message of "Thorpeness" was getting through. It was becoming known - and people liked it. By July there was not an empty bed.

Then, just after the Bank Holiday, on August 4th, the blow came. War was declared against Germany.

Chapter Three

War 1914-1918

STUART Ogilvie was intensely patriotic. He knew the situation was critical when on the fateful Sunday, August 2nd, the Admiralty issued a notice through the Press calling up all classes of Royal Navy Reserves, and some local fishermen left. The following day, the 4th Suffolks, including the famous "H" Company of Leiston and District men, were recalled from their annual training camp and, once war was declared, were sent straight to Colchester for intensive training. Stuart would have enlisted himself, were he

would carry on as usual, and letters were written to clients accordingly. It was felt, however, that the name "Kursaal" with its German connotation, had become undesirable and it was now to be called The Thorpeness Assembly Rooms and Sports Club.

Then the first Zeppelin raid took place over London, where Sholto and Gladys and their little boy and girl lived. Stuart and Helen immediately wrote to both their sons and their daughter Christine saying they would

Sholto Ogilvie on leave in 1916 with (from left to right): Alastair Young (Christine Ogilvie Young's son), Stuart Ogilvie (Alec and Hanna Ogilvie's son), Peggy Ogilvie (Alec and Hanna's daughter), Ailsa Ogilvie (Sholto and Gladys Ogilvie's daughter), Lesley Ogilvie (Alec and Hanna's daughter), Glen (Sholto and Gladys' son)

not too old. He was not surprised, therefore, when both his sons, Alec and Sholto, wrote that they were joining up; nor when some of his work-force did likewise. They were doing the right thing - for King and Country. It was a bitter blow to his plans, though - just when Thorpeness was becoming a reality.

No-one thought the War would last long. "It will be over by Christmas" most people said. Stuart made it known that Thorpeness

like to have their families and look after them until the War was over. They also told their elder son, Alec, that they would stand surety with the authorities for his wife Hanna who was German, so she would not be interned. Sizewell Hall was soon thronging with small children: Alec's Peggy, Lesley and Stuart, Sholto's Glen and Ailsa, and Christine's Alastair. Fortunately, there was no difficulty in finding accommodation for the three separate day and night nurseries, their separate bathrooms, and their nurses and nursemaids.

The Coastal Defences, originally entrusted to the 16 Cyclist 8th Suffolk Regiment, were now reinforced by a Company of Royal Leiston, were in some of the stiffest fighting of the terrible winter of 1914-15 and had suffered heavily, some seventy local casualties being reported. The effect was an even greater rush of recruits wishing to "get out there and bash 'em" from the farms,

Soldiers in the grounds of Sizewell Hall, putting out the fire in 1914

Engineers, quartered locally. Artillery and Anti-Aircraft Units added to the sense of security against possible invasion. Soldiers moved into Sizewell Hall grounds and camped in the rooms under the terrace Stuart had built. Guns and barricades were installed in concrete "pill-boxes" along the cliff and on the common where winding trenches were also dug. Barbed wire entanglements were unrolled along the shore in front of Sizewell Hall and the military took over the Thorpeness Assembly Rooms and many of the houses.

Lord Kitchener's call for recruits had a great response in the locality and recruiting centres became jammed. Autumn came, followed by storms and cold. The 4th Suffolks, including the "H" Company of shops, fishing and factories. The men, grim-faced, went out to hit back.

Building in Thorpeness virtually ceased. Labour was reduced to the old, the medically unfit, or the very young. The possibility of attempted invasion led to the formation of the Voluntary Training Corps (V.T.C.) Leiston, providing a Platoon which soon fitted themselves for eventualities. As the demand for more shells and ammunition came, Richard Garrett & Sons proceeded forthwith to comply with the Government's needs.

For the first time the women and girls straight out of school flocked in to work at the benches. The construction of aeroplanes also started. As a result of the attempted blockade by the Germans with a loss of a number of our ships, every effort was made locally to increase our food supplies. Women again came to the fore and worked with a will, while Boy Scouts, Girl Guides and soldiers home on leave joined in the haymaking and harvesting.

Added to the disappointment of seeing his dream of Thorpeness so cruelly halted, Stuart no longer had the staff to maintain the gardens and houses still in his care as he would have liked, and the presence of soldiers, their horses, gun carriages and wagons, did nothing to enhance the feeling of "peace and harmony" which he had promoted. It was now, also, that he was persuaded to be prudent and change the Company Bank to one in Basle in neutral Switzerland. He did not like it. He felt it showed a lack of faith.

In spite of the War, coastal trading boats and fishermen were still sailing to and fro up the coast and, with violent winter storms, were still getting driven onto the sand banks and wrecked. Then on June 18th 1915, the Liverpool steamboat "Leuctra" was torpedoed and sunk off Aldeburgh. The twenty-four crew were all saved, but the

explosion was heard for miles around. A brigantine, the "Carmenta" was then driven aground between Sizewell Hall and the Ness on February 26th 1916. The sound of the maroon and the sight of distress signals were part of life on the East Coast, and all who could ran to the beach to give a helping hand. This night was one of the worst gales with the heaviest seas on record. The maroon went up at 5.45 a.m., but the Aldeburgh Lifeboat could not get through the immense breakers. The Southwold Lifeboat managed to get under way but could not get near the battered vessel. The "Carmenta" was driven further and further ashore. Meanwhile, as the late Percy Westrup recounted in 1978, the Thorpe Rocket Cart was on the spot and, as one of the crew, he remembered how they managed in spite of the gale to fire a line to the stricken men, and how willing hands on the beach helped them in rescuing all the crew, one by one, by breeches-buoy. (This was a buoyant jacket pulled out to the ship on the rocket string and then to and fro until all were saved). "The sea was terrible," he said.

After all this night of drama, Stuart reviewed the damage done to Thorpeness.

Wreck of the Carmenta, 1915

The strong north-west gale which had raged all night and the scouring of the sea at high tide had completely torn up all the gorse and marram grass that had been planted on the pentlands. A fisherman's hut hung perilously over the miniature cliff, palisading had been undermined and washed down, while one bungalow had been washed away altogether. The Thorpe/Aldeburgh track was flooded and impassable. Tiles were off, old buildings damaged and, as Stuart observed, his tree-planting was a depressing sight. At Aldeburgh, he was told, waves had rushed through the Brudenell Hotel into the High Street. The sea had breached the bank at Slaughden, people were rowing down the High Street, and farmers in boats were rescuing livestock on the marshes. "Things could have been worse" Stuart remarked to Graeme Kemp. "We shall now have to set to and put it right."

At Easter the Meare was opened and advertised as usual, and, in spite of fewer residential visitors, did more business with locals each year. "Happy" Knights and his mate continued to improve, plant, and clear weed on the Meare. By 1916 the reeds had grown and spread to such an extent that they were being cut and sold or used by the estate for thatching. As all the work being done at Thorpeness was anything but cost-effective, they were always looking for a way to "turn a penny". Mrs Naughton's teas at the Boat-house seemed welcome and actually made a small profit. Vegetables from the Hall were sold to the military and Thorpeness, and "Hoppy" Cooper's bee-keeping activities at the Hall with the hundred or so hives were also doing their bit for the war effort (as Hoppy was proud to recount in 1978 when he was in his nineties) "It was my honey, from my li'l owd bees what was the first to be sent out to the sojers at the Front .." he said. "Yeah. Li'l Mrs Ogilvie, she comes to me at the beginning of the War and "Hoppy" she sez, "bring me all you has as I want to send it out to Mr Sholto and the men in the trenches." Mr Sholto allus fancied my honey, he did ... yeah ... and it was my li'l owd bees was the first .." He also looked after the large Belgian hares which were bred in a row of hutches for their meat and for their glossy black fur, skins of which fetched a good price for hat-making.

Sholto Ogilvie and G. Stuart Ogilvie, 1916, at Sizewell Hall

Another season went by. The dreadful war went on. Vital maintenance or alterations were all the Company could manage with the few men available. Meanwhile, Stuart worked away at plans for the future. February 1917 was particularly cold, but a little revenue was made out of advertising skating, charging a shilling a day per person, with soldiers and children half-price. Unfortunately, the weather also meant a spate of burst pipes.

Whitsun Bank Holiday brought record crowds of people to the Meare, and was widely reported in the Press. "Thorpeness once again offered her sea-crowned beauty to refresh and re-fit thousands of war-workers during their brief moment of relaxation.." wrote The East Anglian under the heading "A Day of Diversified Enjoyment"... ending "It is to the children that Thorpeness has always made her greatest call, and once again the little ones prove faithful to their tryst."

In August the London papers and glossy illustrated journals were glad to report the movements of socialites to relieve the relentless gloom of the War. "The popularity of Thorpeness is almost phenomenal" the Tatler wrote, in an effort to reassure their readers that life still went on as normal, with pictures of "The Countess of Essex and her party, the Dowager Countess of Clarendon and family ... Mrs Peel and others," remarking on the popularity of this "Children's Paradise" or "Home of Peter Pan".

Without perhaps realising it, Stuart had struck a note of universal sympathy and approval in being the first person to create a new township, as he sometimes grandly called it, with the main feature in it being for the delight and pleasure of children. Nevertheless, however "normal" and booming Thorpeness was made out to be, from Stuart's angle this was far from the truth. The short summer season was even shorter. July was barely half-full and few people came at all in September. The Assembly Room and many houses were occupied by the Army and could not be let. Meanwhile, the overheads on all the buildings remained. Materials and labour became increasingly difficult.

By 1917, with the appalling death rate at the Front, the older and less fit men were now being called up. Among them was Graeme Kemp (in spite of his weak eyesight) who went into the Motor Transport Army Service Corps in London. Not everyone, too, liked to be reminded by the sounds of war that the battle with all its horrors was so close. The London Press constantly gave detailed reports of the bombardment of East Coast towns, amongst them Yarmouth and Lowestoft. The frequent explosions of mines and torpedoes and the rumble of heavy gun-fire at sea kept war ever in mind. Even the small children at Sizewell got to know the sound of "Big Bertha" across the water, and other weapons. They knew that no chink of light must be shown at night because of "the Germans" - but no suggestion of fear or horror was allowed to reach them.

The raids on the coast were, fortunately, to end abruptly on a night of excitement which has become legend in the district.

"On Sunday morning, June 17, 1917" the Leiston Observer reported, "about 3.15 a.m., the L.48 (one of Count Zeppelin's latest), after being damaged by the fire of the anti-aircraft guns from Felixstowe northwards, was attacked over Leiston by Lieut. F. D. Holder (pilot) and Segt. S. Ashby (gunner) from the Orfordness Aerodrome, and, bursting into flames, fell slowly to earth, finally crashing in a field on Holly Farm, Theberton ... fourteen bodies were removed ... (and now lie in Theberton cemetery)"

It seems that practically every able-bodied man or boy from miles around got there to see the conflagration - and to get some small souvenir. Sholto's wife, Gladys, was presented with a small cross made of charred metal by one of the Sizewell staff who cut across the common on his bike.

Wreck of Zeppelin L48, attacked over Leiston and crashed at Theberton, 17th June 1917

By September 10th when the 159th Thorpeness Advisory Meeting was held the Season was virtually over. No visitors remained. Future bookings were down. Stuart was concerned that the exceptional gales of that week had disturbed many willow stands and white poplars. It was hoped they could be successfully reinstated. Stuart felt gloomy.

By December, following storms and high tides, two new lines of faggoting were made and put along the beach. The Meare was emptied for weed-gathering, digging out and repairing the banks and plantings. The most dispiriting situation which now came to light was the financial one. The accounts showed that although 1917 had been slightly more profitable than previously, the profits were completely nullified by the high rate of interest - 5.5% - charged by the Swiss Bank. This was made even worse by the adverse position of the present rate of exchange. It was decided to let this debt be left, with

interest to accrue, until the end of the War when rates would adjust themselves.

By now the dreadful carnage and the atrocities of war had become continuous facts of life. Older men still, even those with minor disabilities, were being called up for administration work, while the young were being sent out to the Front with the minimal training.

One expected to read, and sorrow for, names of local men killed in action. Men on leave said little about the Front. They were hardened; changed. Stuart and Helen, like other parents, treasured the brief days of leave when their sons came home. They were extremely proud of them. Both had been in constant action: in the Ypres Salient, the Somme, Vimy Ridge, and the worst battlefields. Alec, attached to the 65th Siege Battery, was one of only two Caterpillar Units which had operated continuously. Sholto had risen to be Colonel of his Regiment and had already won the DSO twice for gallantry. The

War could not go on for much longer: Stuart was an optimist. It must end soon. The Germans from all accounts were "finished."

The year went out, regretted by none. It had been a busy year for all those at home. Everyone seemed doing the work of two or more. There was ample opportunity for all to "do their bit". War Relief Committees worked unceasingly and Stuart and Helen played their part. There were fund-raising events of all kinds (many in Thorpeness), comforts for the Services, parcels, sewing-parties, hospital visiting - and some did relief nursing. In addition to running Thorpeness and a large farming estate, Stuart had also been High Sheriff for Suffolk that year and, of course, he had carried on with his designs for the expansion of his "dream", for when peace returned.

New Year 1918 began cold and bleak. Bookings for Easter and the summer, in the houses available, were quite good, all things considered. The Meare re-opened on Good Friday. Few people came down, and due to the wet weather receipts were sparse and no catering undertaken. Following complaints Stuart had made to the Army Officer in command, as to "cruelty to military transport horses on the deep-rutted track from Thorpeness to Aldeburgh, due to the heavy bog" Stuart was able to report to the Advisory Committee on April 6th that the military had decided to construct a road on the Company's land from Thorpeness and then to join up with the hard road just north of the Victoria Jubilee Bridge. He had agreed to supply the military with clay and whin from his adjacent property, free of charge.

Such transactions, however, paled into insignificance the following month when he heard from Gladys that Sholto had been posted "missing". She and the children had gone for their annual month's visit to her parents at Chippenham in Wiltshire. Shortly after, she received a communiqué that he was presumed dead. She refused to believe it, and vehemently proclaimed he was not dead and went on as if nothing had happened. Her mother was much concerned and confided to their Nanny "It's the shock. I'm afraid we must expect a sad reaction soon". It did not come. Meanwhile, Gladys's brother Wallace came home on leave and there was much rejoicing. He had a slight cold but was otherwise well. Within two days he had a raging temperature, became delirious, and died within hours. The doctor diagnosed the virulent influenza ravaging the continent and told Gladys to get the children away as soon as possible. She telegraphed Stuart and Helen who, regardless of the risk, replied "Come at once". The family caught the next train.

A few days later, their Nanny and Gladys's children Glen and Ailsa all had it. A nurse was brought from Ipswich and she and Gladys nursed them day and night. Luckily, baby Fiona and the nursemaid escaped, as did Gladys - strengthened by the firm belief that her brisk walk along the top of the cliff every afternoon blew all germs away. Fortunately, all recovered, but tragically Gladys's two young sisters at Chippenham also caught it and died. Spanish 'flu, as it was now being called, was sweeping Europe, and was said to be killing as many thousands as the War itself.

A month or so later, there was great excitement when Gladys received news that Sholto had been taken prisoner and was in Mainz Jail. He had been helping other prisoners to escape by means of knotted sheets and, as the last to go, was just climbing over the perimeter wall when the moon came out and he was spotted. He had been pursued by guards and dogs, and, as shots were heard Sholto had been presumed dead by his companions who managed to rejoin the British lines. They could not know that he had been put into solitary confinement (with nothing but his vest) in a dungeon. "I knew he was not dead," Gladys said. The relief and joy can be imagined. Once again Stuart felt he could throw himself whole-heartedly into his work. More bookings were coming in

In his weak state Alec had no hope. He succumbed to pneumonia on October 30th 1918. He was thirty-six. The funeral was held in Aldringham on November 5th. The East Anglian gave a full account of the popular and brave Lieutenant, the heir to the estate, and all mourned his death.

Gloom, distraught gloom, enveloped the Ogilvie household, only relieved by the laughter and high-pitched chatter of the little children in their nurseries or as they played innocently in the garden. The routine, too, of their being dressed up after tea every evening to go downstairs (the front stairs!) to play with their mothers and grandmother in the library, was not broken. This always ended with a goodnight visit to Granddad in his study, lit only by the standard lamp by his desk.

November 11th was a day of immense excitement. Suddenly, everyone was smiling. The Nannies, the maids and the staff downstairs seemed to have taken leave of their senses. They were rushing about shouting "Armistice! Armistice has been declared!" waving their arms and throwing their dusters in the air, jumping up and down like jack-in-a-boxes. Sholto's children were being taken out for their afternoon walk (always from the back door), when the cook came running out of the kitchen with a tray full of hot sponge buns, shouting "Catch! It's Armistice! Have an Armistice Bun!" She appeared to be quite hysterical. The children gathered that this weird behaviour and strange word had something to do with the War being over and everyone coming home - but Armistice to them meant a delicious, hot, squishy bun.

including some notable people, such as the Asquiths. His old optimism was returning.

Shortly afterwards, a telegram arrived for Hanna saying Alec had been wounded and was being brought home. That was good news. They did not realise *how* he was coming home ... he arrived blinded and unconscious at the First London General Hospital at Camberwell, suffering from mustard gas. Through the next agonising weeks, with the skill of doctors and nurses, Alec's eyesight began to return. His painful, damaged lungs were much improved. He was daily getting stronger, and was allowed to get up. Then the dreaded Spanish 'flu struck.

Chapter Four

Peace and Progress - Disaster

THE War had been grinding on for so long that people had got used to shortages, to food rationing, long hours of work for the war effort and also to the comradeship of common purpose and "pulling together". If anyone thought that once hostilities ceased and the men returned from the trenches life would return to how it had been before the War, they were in for a severe shock. Shortages, if anything, became even greater, with more people home to feed. Industrial supplies, geared for the war machine, had to adjust. The heroes returned to the "land fit for heroes", as promised. But they found it was not. Many were sick, shell-shocked, limbless, or maimed. They were not the same men that went out there. They had changed. Also they found all too often that their wives or girl-friends had changed. They had got used to their independence. For the first time, women had been earning good money - on munitions, in the factory, or on the land. And they wanted to carry on. Factories, however, if not closing altogether, were cutting down until the Peace Treaty was finally signed, and the women were the first to be laid off.

Wages had risen sharply and would never return to pre-war levels. The Government controlled all industrial and building materials which were so scarce that free enterprise development virtually ceased. Stuart, however, was determined that nothing would stop him from pursuing once more the plans for his "dream". Meanwhile, the soldiers were still in occupation in Thorpeness Assembly Rooms and Sports Club and a number of other houses, and were going to remain there until Peace was signed:

the only good thing was that they were building the road to Aldeburgh. The buildings would then all have to be renovated and re-decorated. The frustration was maddening - and depressing.

The death of Alec weighed heavily upon the Ogilvie family. Sholto came home in poor health, very thin and with gastric trouble following his solitary confinement in the cold dungeon. He was practically starved. Without the little food gifts from friends, pushed in under the ill-fitting door, he doubted if he would have survived. He had now received a second bar to his DSO and Stuart was very proud of him. Very proud.

As his workmen returned, he welcomed them all back, and others who had served their King and Country - some of whom were disabled. All were given jobs and set to work to smarten up the village for the 1919 long-awaited peacetime Season. It was hoped that, in spite of shortages, more bungalows would be ready for use in July. The new Universal Stores was opened to supply every requirement for the visitors and received its off-licence for wines and spirits in June. The Press was full of its future plans. Spring and Summer came, but the soldiers still had not left. "The hamlet still shows rough treatment at the hands of the soldiery", The East Anglian said, "and although the Sports Club buildings were not yet available, the tennis courts would be renovated in a fortnight." The London and major provincial Press and the fashionable Illustrated Chronicle, Tatler, Sketch and others dwelt much on the social scene with lists of eminent people who had discovered this "select new resort" which was so completely different from anywhere else. The gossip writers showed pictures of house-parties, including Lord Blandford, Lady Essex, Lady Cynthia and Alexandra Curzon, Lady Mavyth Ward and many others who had "returned to their bungalows for a month or so ..." However, Thorpeness was not only for the socialites. Outings of the Girls' Friendly Society, Boy Scouts, children and clubs by the Great Eastern Railway were also reported, and people from Aldeburgh and local surrounding villages had come in greater numbers than ever before, thanks to the new road.

The short Season, in fact, went extremely well. Even September, until the private school holidays ended, had been over half-full. The costs, though, were heavy. Everywhere had needed re-painting and renovating. Financially, the truth could hardly give cause for elation. There was, however, War Reparation and Compensation to look forward to. Everyone was well satisfied. Thorpeness was getting back on its feet.

The next two years showed a steady improvement of facilities. The Army, thankfully, finally left in 1920, and Stuart decided to enlarge and improve the Club, and call it The County Sports Club. It would be re-opened in 1921. Meanwhile, everyone in the village was delighted when in April 1920 Alfred Alexander was among those in the King's Honours List to receive the MBE for services rendered as a coast watcher during the War. He was sixty-two, and it cited his twenty-six years in the Thorpeness Lifeboat, including eight years as coxswain upon the retirement of his father who had been coxswain of the same boat for forty years! It mentioned that Alfred saw the tragic drama of a merchant vessel being torpedoed by a German submarine just north of the Ness, and had also spotted a number of floating mines.

May 1921 saw the formation of Thorpeness Cricket Club on land which Stuart donated. An old railway carriage was converted as the first pavilion. A number of longshore fishermen and others joined, and a strong eleven was formed who played Thorpeness v. The Visitors, and also against other villages. May was hot and sunny, and June was one of the hottest and driest on record. Thorpeness was again looking beautiful with flowers everywhere. The trees and shrubs, now well-established, were in full, fresh leaf, and the broom and gorse on the commons were a blazing gold. As July proceeded and the sun ever shone, the farmers bewailed the drought. Stuart sympathised with his farm manager, but his heart was in Thorpeness and he rejoiced at the stifling heat which was bringing the crowds flocking to find a sea breeze, to bathe on the sandy beach, or to enjoy the cool waterways of the Meare.

July 15th was the day of the official re-opening of the Thorpeness County Sports Club by the Lady Huntingfield. The new Lord Huntingfield, who had recently succeeded to the title, was also present, together with members of his family and a long list of what was described as "distinguished personalities from the County".

The enlarged Club included what Stuart described as the "Cantonment". This was a 'wheeze' he had to enable the Company to house more people than the Club could accommodate - such was the overwhelming demand. He had had Graeme Kemp purchase the redundant wooden army huts from Hazlewood and Woodbridge and re-erect them in gardens on the Uplands, with specific instructions to arrange them 'artistically' with gables here and there and some sideways on so no two should look exactly alike. Some were already occupied by estate workers, the rest were now set aside for Club members and their families pending the building of the Club Dormy House. They would be lodged there and catered for at the Club on very moderate inclusive terms. "This arrangement" it averred "which solves the servant problem will be much appreciated." It was.

Stuart, determined that visitors to Thorpeness would find everything to their liking, had a paper given to every member of the Club and all the visitors at the end of the last Season, asking for their criticisms or suggestions on a list of items. The result had been almost universally satisfactory. Some of the young, however, had said there was not much doing at night. This was now, therefore, going to be remedied. The new 1921 booklet called "Concerning Thorpeness" announced their Fixture List for 1921, beginning with the opening of the new enlarged clubhouse to visitors on July 11th and a County Subscription Ball on July 22nd; there would be Weekend Dances (open to non-residents) in August and September, Flannel Cinderella Dances (members only) throughout the Season, Thé Dansants on Saturday afternoons in the Theatre, Foxtrot Competitions under the direction of Miss Gwendoline Palmer, August and September. There would also be Subscription Concerts, and Mr Webster Millar, the brilliant operatic tenor, would give first class concerts, supported by his colleagues of the Beecham Opera Company and well-known instrumentalists, commencing August 3rd. There would be weekly whist drives (members only), a Venetian Fête and a Feast of Lanterns on the Meare, with special prizes for the best-decorated and illuminated craft, in August. Also in August, Mr Louis N. Parker would organise Amateur Dramatics and performances (stage manager: Major Clarke-Jervoise), including a children's ballet under the direction of Madame Edith Baird (first performance: August 22nd) Tennis Tournaments (open to all comers) would be held throughout August, and there would be a Meare Regatta with special prizes for juvenile sailing and rowing events. In September there would be a military band and fireworks.

The members were delighted. There was something for everyone - even amateur dramatics which were all the vogue at the time and which those who wished could join in. There was nowhere - nowhere at all - like Thorpeness.

The stifling heat wave continued. The grass was scorched, and everything was tinder dry. All arrangements had been made for the first dance of the Season, July 22nd. Stuart and Helen were expecting all their family and grandchildren (now nine of them) at the Hall for the summer, but the late Alec's three children and Alastair, Christine's boy, were not arriving until the next week, like Glen, after their schools broke up. Then on the morning of the dance, out of the clear blue sky, disaster struck this happy family home.

A spark from the kitchen chimney fell on the thatch and, in spite of being noticed at 10.30 a.m. and (it was thought) extinguished by gardeners with ladders and buckets of water, travelled under the roof and burst out all over the east end. It was eleven o'clock: the children and their nurse, with Gladys, were on the beach at the time. When they realised what was happening, they hurried up the cliff. The fire rapidly became an inferno. The full force of the Leiston Works Fire Brigade was called, both the manual engine and the steamer. Three jets from each were used from the ornamental lake, but it was evident that the house was doomed although there were plenty of onlookers to man the pumps. "In actual fact" the Leiston Observer reported "there was a delay in the horses being released from other duties and the horsemen did not want them overtaxed by hard driving in the heat, so it was three-quarters of an hour before they arrived. (These fire engines may now be seen in The Long Shop Museum, Leiston). "The sight of the flames brought literally hundreds of people to the site - by cars, vans, horse-drawn vehicles and on foot" it continued. "They picnicked on the lawns, they explored the gardens, and among the 'helpers' were those who came to pick up what they could."

Nevertheless, nothing would deter G. Stuart Ogilvie from proceeding with everything as planned for the Opening Ball at the Country Club (as it is now called). Meanwhile, arrangements were being made in the courtyard for sorting. Fortunately, the Fire Brigade had concentrated on preventing the fire spreading further and damping down the adjacent flames. Even so, the fire blazed all day, and at night the ground floor was still glowing hotly among the few remaining chimney stacks.

Leiston Works Fire Brigade tackles the flames in 1921 as workers help to salvage the furniture

to move the entire household, taking everything they needed that they could rescue to Cliff House nearby, which fortunately was both empty and partially furnished.

"The feeling of gloom which prevailed earlier in the day in Thorpeness" the Observer continued "evaporated when Mr Ogilvie arrived and expressed the wish that his great loss was not to make any difference but he regretted that his house-party could not be present as intended." Indeed they spent the day rescuing paintings, valuables and belongings, as much as could be done before the entire roof fell in. If they had any suitable clothes rescued, they were probably among the stacks of furniture, linen and objets d'art still on the lawn or being taken to buildings

The family, guests and entire indoor and outdoor staff had worked all day, rescuing belongings, furniture and works of art - including the Blüthner concert grand piano, harp, and valuable chinoiserie from the upstairs drawing-room. Sholto directed the salvage operation which went quickly and with the precision of a well-rehearsed military exercise. When it became too dangerous to continue upstairs, the men there joined the downstairs teams putting everything in piles on the lawn. Here, Gladys's brother-in-law, Captain Geoffrey Watkins, RN (who was a very powerful man) guarded the goods from would-be pilferers until they could be moved to the stables and outhouses for sorting and storing. He actually

Sizewell Hall, gutted and guarded by police

caught two men in the act of removing a valuable piece of furniture towards their handy van and banged their heads together with such force that it took some time before they came round (as he recounted). Then the fire engines and police arrived and the sightseers were driven back.

Meanwhile, others of the household staff had gone over to Cliff House to prepare it for the influx of people - house-party, children and staff. The house was cleaned, the range lighted. Henry, the coachman, plied to and fro with the gig taking all that would be needed so at least everyone would have somewhere to sleep and something to eat. Blankets were sorted, rooms allotted, crockery and cooking utensils brought over, and the larder filled. Fortunately the back or west end of the house was kept clear of the fire.

Everywhere an air of suppressed excitement and purposeful bustling prevailed. It was a momentous day. We,

Sholto's children, were taken by Nanny with a piled-up pram to Sizewell Gap and left with Mrs Ryder, the doctor's wife. It was my duty, at nearly eight years old, to help Mrs Ryder and to keep the three younger ones happy. Bruce was only six months old (guarding my mother's jewellery under his pillow); Griselda, two and a half, and Fiona, five. They seemed to sense the "emergency." They all behaved beautifully. We lived on bread and jam, and cheese - for the first time, as in our household it was considered indigestible for children. We ate it, but we did not like it. We also had to drink quantities of tepid, scalded milk (which we hated) but nobody complained. As the sun was sinking we were collected and taken to Cliff House where Fiona and I were put on one mattress on the bare floor in an attic. Two other mattresses were to be occupied by our own nursemaid and a kitchen maid and two other young maids. We had one blanket, and we slept in our vests. There was no light except for the

fading red sky through a small skylight window. Far below, we could hear the creaking rhythm of the two men pumping the water up from the well beneath the motionless American Windmill, and the gentle splash as it fell into the water-tank outside our door. No wonder we slept soundly.

The Season of Thorpeness proceeded without a hitch, unaffected by the drama and aftermath of the 'Great Fire'. The programme

*The Ogilvie family the day after the
fire pictured at Cliff House. From top
left: Captain Watkins, Sholto Ogilvie,
Helen Ogilvie; centre: Gladys Ogilvie,
Alastair Young, Fiona Ogilvie, Ailsa Ogilvie;
from top right: Phyllis Watkins, G. Stuart
Ogilvie, Christine (Ogilvie) Alcock*

Some of the Sizewell Hall staff, the day after the fire. Back row: _____, Roberta Meadows (cook), George Edworthy (Chauffeur), Nora (under-nurse); front row: Hilda (parlour maid), Elsie Finch (under-nurse), Bertha (head Housemaid)

of events was acclaimed an unqualified success. The County Ball was packed with "landowners and local gentry bringing parties from far and near". The concerts were of a quality not hitherto experienced in this area. Stuart was understandably jubilant.

In September, at the end of an undoubtedly successful season, Stuart could report to his fellow directors that he anticipated he would receive £18,000 from the Royal Exchange Assurance Company, following the disastrous burning down of Sizewell Hall. He wished to start rebuilding as soon as possible and he had accepted the tender from Thorpeness building team. It was noticed that there would be no work for the carpenters for at least eight weeks. Work, therefore, would have to be found for them. He then produced the plans for a wooden annexe or 'dormy-house' for the Club, to be approached by a covered way, and it was resolved that the carpenters should be put onto this.

The Royal Exchange were slow in sending a cheque, and wrote quibbling letters. However, the expected letter finally arrived. Sholto was there. Stuart opened it and then fell into a towering rage, swearing like a trooper: "£10,000! A piffling ... blank blank blankety ... £10,000 ... It's an insult to my intelligence ... the blank ... crooked, fraudulent so and so's, etc. etc." and with a gesture worthy of Sir Henry Irving, he dramatically tore the cheque in half. If they did not pay him in full, he would have their despicable dishonesty blazed across every newspaper in London... He wrote a ferocious letter, enclosing the two halves of the cheque.

To see such an enormous cheque treated with such contempt shook Sholto rigid. He knew, however, that if Stuart had kept the cheque it would be taken that it was accepted as payment in full. Stuart won the day: he got the full amount! Work started. It had been an eventful year.

Chapter Five

The Great Building Programme

STUART and Helen remained at Cliff House, their family and the grandchildren having returned to their own homes after the summer holiday. It was exposed to every wind, shabby, furnished for holiday use only, and so cold that even the oil lamps and candles were welcome for added warmth.

Harry Kemp having retired, the farms were now under the management of Mr Joseph Dorrington, who had previously been a tenant who farmed Scot's Hall. He was not popular among the other employees. He was, however, 'a gentleman'. A large florid man, genial, flattering and a good shot, he managed the shoots reasonably well - which is what interested Stuart most. Stuart was so taken up with plans for Thorpeness that he was glad to leave the farming to Dorrington, assuming that he would be as efficient and trustworthy as Harry Kemp had been.

Now the effects of the aftermath of the War were easing up, Stuart could not wait to resume the major developments he had planned. With the building team involved in rebuilding the Hall, he decided to create the nine hole golf links. With this in mind, James Braid, the most famous of golf course designers, agreed to come and inspect the proposed site and lay out a draft plan for nine holes for the fee of £12 plus expenses, the work to be extended to eighteen holes the following year. The nine hole course was scheduled to open in August 1922.

It is unnecessary to go into all the details of the financial transactions the directors had to arrange in order to finance the programme they had set themselves. Stuart pledged his own £16,000 worth of War Loan Bonds to the Company in return for 4% Debenture Stock to the value of £14,880. This obtained for them from Barclays Bank, Ipswich, an overdraft up to £10,000. They also closed their bank account in Switzerland, where they had reached their limit of overdraft.

In April 1922, the East Anglian reported the inaugural meeting of the Thorpeness Golf Club which would be affiliated to the County Sports Club, with a list of members and officers. The first ten holes, designed by James Braid and completed under the supervision of John L. Cassidy (who for fifteen years was the popular professional of the famous Aldeburgh Club), would be opened on July 1st: the other eight holes of the 8,000 yards course, by the spring of 1923. A commodious wooden Golf Pavilion where refreshments would be served would be built behind The Mart, and a Caddy House beside it by the Aldringham Road. This would enable it to be open all the year round. The annual subscriptions were fixed pro tem at £3 for gentlemen and £2 for ladies. The children of Thorpeness residents only, between the ages of 12 and 18, would pay £1 11s. 6d. Green fees were set at three shillings and sixpence except from mid-July to mid-September, when they would be five shillings. The President, Mr G. Stuart Ogilvie, said that for the first year members of the Country Club who were founder members of the Golf Club would not have to pay a subscription.

The 1922 Season went with a swing but with very different weather from the hot drought of the previous year. Golf and cricket were popular added amenities, and the newspapers made much of the Annual Regatta in August. The gossip writers were busy with their cameras of 'notable' jolly family parties, such as the four pretty little daughters of Lady Violet Gregson, Lord Lichfield's sister, and Lady Emily Lytton and family, and the Regatta prizes for decorated boats being judged by the Hon. Mrs Bertrand Sackville-West and Mrs H. R. Tollemache.

More important to the permanent residents, however, was that Thorpeness Halt now boasted a waiting-room. The Great Eastern had fitted out a smart old railway carriage on the platform with one-man porter, ticket-collector, clerk, station master - who obligingly also dealt with advance luggage, goods and local parcels.

The building of the Hall was going on at amazing speed. In fact, this large house, with guest suites replacing the nurseries, and with twenty-two bedrooms and nine bathrooms, was already looking nearly finished. The reason for this remarkable progress was the equally remarkable fact that it was being constructed (with the exception of the chimneys) entirely out of concrete slabs, made on the site in wooden forms by unskilled labour. Not being allowed to replace the roof with thatch by the insurance companies, Stuart chose his favourite Jacobean style, with high pitched gables of different sizes, richly carved oak barge-boards and finials, and thick-ribbed brown mottled Cornish slates. Faithful reproduction of old oak carving was made on the fascia boards and on the transoms of the leaded windows. The half timber work had artificially-produced sun-cracks and weathering while the studied unevenness of the surface work, with rough tool marks on the plaster skin, all suggested "a long-lost period" Stuart wrote in his 'Concerning Thorpeness' (1925) "before the individuality and loving art of the craftsman had been blotted out by the damnable reiteration of standardised and machine-made goods".

Luckily, Thorpeness had - and prized - her craftsmen, and it would not be long now before his "beautiful old oak-panelled dining-room" was finished.

Meanwhile, Stuart and Helen welcomed all their family and grandchildren back with them for the next summer holidays at Cliff House and its annexe over the garages.

With the concrete slab-making at the Hall having come to an end and having proved so successful, Stuart decided to have the work continued at Ted's Barn, half-way along the cliff to Thorpeness. Hayward & Sons of Saxmundham were therefore asked to quote for sinking a deeper well there than the one sunk for Stuart's mother's stock-yard. With so many huge capital expenses before them and with such a short season to pay for it all, the aim of the Company was to let properties more and more on long leases to extend the length of time people stayed in the village in order to bring in revenue. The financial statement in November 1922 showed an overdraft at the Bank of £11,872. There were also the mortgages with the Building Societies. Nevertheless, Stuart was pleased with the year, all things considered. He now looked forward to moving into the Hall with its central heating in time for Christmas, although it was still not finished.

In spite of the constant difficulty of cash-flow - always a problem in a rapidly expanding company - Stuart was determined to go full steam ahead with his building programme. First priority was the water supply.

It was then that he saw the opportunity of acquiring what he had always dreamed of - a picturesque old windmill. Since the miller at Aldringham had retired, the old corn mill on Mill Hill had ceased to turn. Stuart made enquiries, and was able to purchase it. His advisers (as reported in the Minutes of their weekly meetings) were dead against it. "Madness! Useless! A waste of money!" they cried. There were far cheaper and more efficient ways of pumping!

Aldringham Mill about 1890.

"It is a thing of beauty!" Stuart replied. "It will enhance the village." He then announced that he also had a novel plan for a new larger water tower to replace the hideous 10,000 gallon 'New Mill' which was now inadequate. And on April 10th 1923 (the Minutes recorded) "it was advised that a new water tower with a capacity of at least 30,000 gallons be erected near the New Mill and that such tower be so constructed as to be ornamental as well as providing living accommodation therein ..." A letter was dictated to Mr Forbes Glennie asking him immediately to prepare plans etc. for the erection of the water tower in steel and wood on the lines indicated by the sketches prepared by the Chairman. Meetings became contentious.

Those present were not impressed and were highly dubious that anyone would want to live beneath 30,000 gallons of water

pumping up and down, let alone in this extraordinary edifice - but Stuart was adamant. "A village needs character and features", he maintained, "not just houses." Other plans for Thorpeness included plans for laying new water mains and for looking into the question of putting in a main sewerage system.

The steel work of the "Gazebo" (as Stuart had named the new water tower house) was being erected by Messrs Bawn & Braithwaite, and it was nearly completed by September. They had been informed that speed was of the essence, but Stuart was becoming increasingly impatient with Forbes Glennie who seemed loath to answer his frequent letters asking to be sent the completed plans. In fact, Forbes Glennie probably hoped that the whole mad idea would be dropped and was reluctant to be associated with it.

The Season had gone well, with every available bed let and the Press giving wide coverage to the what were already becoming Annual Events - the Meare, the Regatta, happy family groups, golf, and entertainments - and the cheerfulness and personal service given by the staff was remarked on by visitors as a special feature of Thorpeness. Stuart liked to show his appreciation to his staff and workmen, and on September 29th 1923 the Leiston Observer gave a report of the Thorpeness Ltd Outing at the close of the holiday season when "a party of sixty were conveyed by Eastern County Road Car Company to Lowestoft" (it said) "... after a substantial lunch, the Chairman, Mr G. Stuart Ogilvie, referred to the extraordinary development of Thorpeness and its growing popularity ... He was profuse in his expressions of gratitude to all those who had honestly and loyally put in a fair day's work for a fair day's pay... Their wages were not high ... they had realised the position ..."

Mr T. Morley, Managing Director, pointed out that Mr Ogilvie, too, had done his part and had "backed his own judgement to the extent of nearly £800,000 - and had lost a good proportion of it. It had cost Mr Ogilvie no less than £30,000 to maintain the development since the War began and, naturally, it was not yet able to pay its way." He added that it illustrated the immense good which can be achieved when employers and employees work in a spirit of confidence and co-operation for the good of the object. A pleasant journey to Yarmouth, the matinée performance at the Regal Theatre and a good tea followed, after which the party left at 9 pm for home.

For the summer of 1924 the bookings were again good. Publicity was excellent, and everyone was happy. Nevertheless, it was apparent that the ambitious building programme set out by Stuart would have to be curtailed. The old windmill, dating from 1803, had been beautifully restored and converted to pumping water from the well up into the 70 ft high 30,000 gallon tank now erected in the almost completed water tower - referred to variously in the Press as "Water Tower Bungalow", "Reservoir Villa", and as "a highly picturesque and unique landmark."

More and more people who could not rent a house were booking into the Country Club with their nurses and children. Stuart, though delighted to see them, realised it could become a problem if the place became overrun with little ones - particularly at meal-times if it was impossible to find a quiet seat. Furthermore, they were on reduced rates. He, therefore, had planned a novel idea of an extension to the Club to be called 'Juvenalia' to house and cater for children separately. This, sadly, he had to postpone too. It was agreed, however,

that 'The Tea House' (now Sandy Lodge) on the Benthills could go ahead at a cost of £500. This, together with alteration and maintenance jobs and switching some of the labour force to making gardens, roads and the laying of new plumbing, would keep everyone in employment until the next big projects could be tackled. These were to be the building of the Almshouses for retired estate workers, and the Workmen's Club - always provided that the Company could obtain the contracts in open competition. The funding for these would come from the money left by his mother for charitable purposes and which had been accumulating in the hands of the Charity Commissioners.

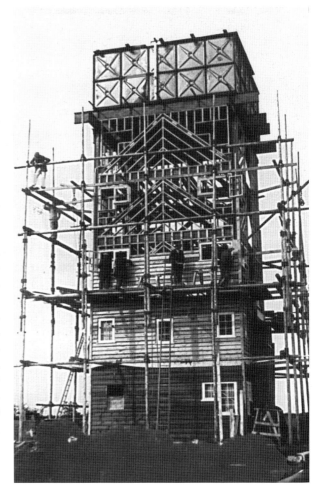

A start is made on the "Gazebo" - later to be named "The House in the Clouds"

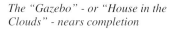

hundred strong sat down to a dinner in the ballroom of the Country Club, followed by a highly entertaining concert. Stuart's speech included a diatribe against the Government and its crushing taxation which had the effect of drying up surplus capital ... if he had to stop building it would mean laying off men. Fortunately they had just secured (in open competition against some of the biggest building firms in England) a contract to build the Alexander Ogilvie Workmen's Club at Thorpeness, but they had to cut prices to the very bone and to charge nothing for all the work at the office.

Stuart now put practically his entire workforce onto building. He hoped also to get Juvenalia ready for the next season. He could now keep everyone employed throughout the winter. The concrete slab factory at Ted's Barn took advantage of the presence of shingle and sharp sand on the spot. The deep well with American windmill was working (supplemented with a petrol engine if insufficient wind) and also the aerial bucket line for hauling shingle up the cliff and depositing it in the tip-up wagons over the tramway lines now set up (which were first used by Stuart's father across the Meare, taking ballast for his railway line to Aldeburgh).

A siding stood to the west side of the present Almshouses. From here, Portland Cement, which was collected by lorry from Thorpeness Halt, was loaded onto the wagons and drawn by horse to the factory. Likewise, the slabs were brought down on flat trucks to be collected either for use on

Although the Season had started off wet and cold and early takings were disastrously down, fortunately the weather changed and late July and August were hot and sunny. Golf, cricket, tennis, the Meare and the children's Regatta all flourished, and Stuart was always proud (in spite of his wry remarks!) to see his grandchildren among the prize-winners. The dances were as popular as ever, and brought in parties from Aldeburgh and the surrounding country. On September 24th, when the Season was over, the East Anglian and the Leiston Observer again gave a long report on Thorpeness Ltd entertaining its workforce. This time a the adjacent sites or by lorry for Juvenalia or housing. The Company had already metalled over 5,850 yards of private roads, most of which were also tarred and curbed - as Graeme Kemp records in his Minutes.

Stuart was proud that the Company had settled amicably the two vexed questions of Dilution and Continuity of Employment which (as he wrote in his "Concerning Thorpeness," 1925) "the mighty Trades Unions, with all their paralysing strikes and suicidal strife, have been unable to solve. Our skilled tradesmen recognise that without the free dilution of unskilled labour their work would automatically cease, and they welcome the assistance of untrained men." Local fishermen, in bad weather, had often been thankful for this source of work. Furthermore, priority was always given to those who had 'served their country in its hour of need' - not that those on vital munitions and the land had not - but of his building operatives Stuart took pride that 83% were ex-service men and 28% more or less disabled by the War, and also that even in the peculiarly unfavourable climatic conditions of the winter of 1923-4 not one member of the staff was stood off for a single day. By the careful pre-arrangement of each

year's operations, work under cover as well as in the open meant that (provided workers were not tied by trades union rules) continuity of employment was assured.

People were astonished at the way buildings were going up, gardens established and, always, trees being planted or replaced if failed. In spite of Stuart openly bemoaning that "money was the problem" in such a huge undertaking and rapid expansion, the locals never really believed him. They saw his big shooting parties, his house guests of well-known people - politicians, judges, lawyers, writers, and wealthy landowners who were frequently shown the progress made in his 'dream village' - and they heard of the sumptuous table he kept and his love of good wines and old port, and perhaps understandably thought his wealth was a bottomless pit. "There he sits! Dazed with rich food!" wrote the acrimonious communist columnist on the Leiston Observer in one of his tirades. This caused great hilarity and became an heirloom catch phrase sometimes even used today if someone is thought to have over-indulged.

It was the cash flow problem, however, which still dominated the Directors' meetings. It was decided, therefore, to obtain

Westbar in 1924 with "The House in the Clouds" in the distance

further capital by offering long leaseholds for cash premiums, together with a nominal ground rent of £1 per annum. The first tenant in the 'Gazebo' (depicted in the 1925 "Concerning Thorpeness") was Mrs Malcolm Mason and her family. She was a writer of children's stories and poems, and when Stuart heard she had written a poem on her "House in the Clouds", he said he would very much like to see it and invited her to lunch. So delighted was he with the name that he said that from henceforth it would be called "The House in the Clouds" and she would be his "Lady of the Stairs and Starlight." The Masons lived happily there until all the children were grown up and married, after the Second World War.

The novel conception of Juvenalia, which was officially opened on July 3rd 1925, received wide acclaim. "A Children's Club" said the Daily Mail "... their own club at Thorpeness, the Suffolk Coast children's paradise ... bedrooms, a matron, rooms for nurses and children or parents who wish to sleep near their children..." "Parents' Problems Solved" were the headlines in the Morning Post, while the Daily Telegraph extolled the virtues of "the prettiest and most peaceful of seaside villages" and announced the "notable addition of the new children's wing, complete with their own refectory, playroom and dormitories for forty children and their attendants". The East Anglian and Leiston Observer, needless to say gave full coverage of the event, including Lord Huntingfield's speech in which he said he had a particular interest in Thorpeness since his predecessor had parted with all rights of wreck on the foreshore - the manorial rights.

The Season was soon in full swing, and Juvenalia was a resounding success from the start. It was a completely new and untried idea. Parents loved it, nurses were thankful they could actually do washing there or use a little pantry for preparing special foods, and the children thought it wonderful, too. Everyone seemed to make friends immediately. Old clients returned. New people came. Thorpeness was so different - so lovely, they said. Without realising it, it had become a 'cult' place. Stuart walked round the Club practically every day. He chatted with people, asked their views, sought their advice, He noticed everything: a rambler rose needed tying back, a shrub wanted watering, an extra vase of flowers would look well in a corner. He would see that more flowers were sent tomorrow from the Hall. He watched the tennis. The eight new 'Grassphalte' courts were very popular, and needed no upkeep. The terraced grandstand seating by the 'Centre Court' was another amenity much appreciated, and made a good place for the presentation of prizes. Unfortunately, though, such refinements brought in no extra revenue.

Despite the cold, wet September which affected all holiday resorts, the result of the year's trading had broken all previous records. Stuart was glad, therefore, to be able to tell his workforce at the end of season dinner and concert that "inasmuch as every penny of profit was re-invested for further development, it meant more work for the employees." He spoke quite openly of the hard times being experienced by all businesses in the difficult post-war era, excessively high rates and taxes making funding and obtaining extra capital very difficult. This keeping the workers in the picture was almost unique at this time, particularly by a landowner. The men appreciated it and, as Thorpeness Ltd foreman Mickey Staff said (in 1977, when nearly 78), "You could always go to him and he would always listen. He was always very fair. If there were two of you who disagreed went along, he listened to both sides and you both came away feeling he done you fair. Very fair, he was."

It worried Stuart that the years were fleeing past. "There is so much, so much to do," he often said despondently. In his "Concerning Thorpeness", 1925, in his somewhat wordy political chapter on private enterprise and how it had been proved to work, he described the many achievements of Thorpeness Ltd which, in spite of war difficulties, was a remarkable feat of co-operation. The achievements included: buying 380 acres of land, creating the Meare, building 120 holiday homes, the Country Club, the Universal Store, the Golf Links and Pavilions; installing gas, and water - sinking wells and building towers and laying over three miles of pipes; sewerage, the daily collection of refuse and cess-pits regularly emptied; purchase and practically re-building of the village inn; laying out and planting over a hundred gardens and five acres of cliff terraced gardens; building garaging for 46 cars and two large covered yards for 30 more; also livery stables containing both motor and horse-drawn vehicles; making a cricket field with pavilion (an old railway carriage renovated), the concrete factory with 1,780 yards of tramway lines and sidings, the roads - over 5,850 yards metalled - and, of course, the continual planting and tending of trees and shrubs of which a quarter of a million had already been put in. All this being completed in spite of one year being taken off for the re-building of Sizewell Hall, gave him good reason to be fairly satisfied - but he could not wait to press on with the next phase.

The news at the October Directors' Meeting was not good. The overdraft was £17,416, without the interest on it of approximately £3,000. Mr Morley, the Managing Director, was leaving. Stuart proposed that a voluntary gift of £500 be paid to him for his service. A Mr Roy Wilson was taking his place. A Captain Valentine Fox was also appointed, as Secretary of the Golf and County Sports Club, at a salary of £156 per annum and rent-free occupation of 'Alexandra House', Thorpeness. This was the cottage Alfred Alexander had once occupied: the name change to 'Alexandra' seems to have been adapted by the office to avoid

confusion. Needless to say, the locals never used it.

Stuart had been negotiating with two different concerns who were willing to put quite substantial sums into the Company and take an active interest. It turned out that in each case they would virtually want a free hand or overriding control, and this was unthinkable. Without further capital, however, building would have to stop. Stuart therefore announced in November that he was prepared to pay off the Company's entire overdraft at the Bank up to £20,000, and take in return £20,000-worth of First Mortgage Debentures. Barclays Bank agreed to continue mortgage facilities and the programme of building set forth.

The farming side of the estate had long been giving cause for concern. Stuart had never had time for detailed supervision of this. On being questioned closely, Mr Joseph Dorrington retired from his managing directorship of Sizewell Farms Ltd. - ostensibly owing to failing health. Stuart, who wished the "retirement" to be peaceable, gave a luncheon for him at Sizewell Hall, inviting his successor, Capt. J. R. Taylor, together with Sholto and the chief officers of Thorpeness Ltd. Stuart thanked Dorrington warmly for his work, and presented him with an inscribed silver rose-bowl. He said they were all aware of the disastrous period through which British agriculture was passing, and for the last nine years, with the exception of the financial year just closed, far from making any just return on the large amount of capital employed, they had nothing but disappointment and financial losses. Joseph Dorrington, always cheery, always undaunted, only now on the eve of his departure had been able to produce a balance sheet which showed a profit. Sholto, who had been asked to analyse the state of the Com-panies and who had already put some probing questions to Dorrington and made critical remarks to him, would not have been so kind.

Chapter Six

The Book - Sorrow and Change

FOLLOWING his detailed examination of all aspects of running this large and complex estate and the introduction of both the new manager of Sizewell Farms Ltd and the new Managing Director of Thorpeness Ltd, Sholto suggested the introduction of a Progress Book. This would mean that Stuart, instead of leaving chits of paper at the office with comments or directions to the various heads of departments, should write them all in one large book for channelling through to the Managing Director, who would then make his brief comment on the opposite page. Thus Stuart would be fully informed and a check could be made that each point had been satisfactorily dealt with. Any suggestions from heads of departments, too, could be included in the Book and answered by the Managing Director. Sholto ran this system in his own London office where he was joint Managing Director of The National Gas Council, (now British Gas).

Stuart's first official chit to the Managing Director, Mr Roy Wilson, set down that once the organisation and co-ordination of the executive side of the business had been perfected, he wished him to concentrate on the vital matters of finance and future developments. Once every week Stuart would receive a cash statement, and, monthly, a very full statement. He would also receive a short programme of work carried out that month, and working schemes as to the next month's plans.

Stuart was full of optimism. The new overdraft with the Bank having been agreed, work on the farms and Thorpeness was going ahead with added vigour under the new management. In spite of winter weather, by February (1926) the Almshouses and the maintenance work were well ahead. Then on February 18th, Stuart received a most devastating blow.

Helen, who was prone to bronchitis, had also had one or two bouts of trouble with her heart over the past years. She had been driven out on Wednesday morning (as was her habit, to visit workers' wives, look at projects in hand or to shop) and on her return was not feeling well and went to bed. She died of a heart attack in her sleep early on Thursday morning. Stuart could not believe it: he was stunned. Heartbroken.

Sholto received the news at breakfast time at his home in Surrey. Strangely enough, it was not such an unexpected shock to the household as might be thought. Certainly the maids awaited a telegram's arrival. For, at about four in the morning, there had been a resounding crash, and it was found that the large oil painting of the Madonna (in a particularly heavy ornate frame) had fallen off the wall on the landing. The whole household rushed out to see what had happened, and as soon as Nanny saw it she exclaimed "Someone has died!" The maids all murmured in agreement. "Nonsense!" Gladys had said "I expect the cord has broken." It had not, but the nail had come out of the wall, bringing some plaster with it.

The funeral took place at Aldringham the following week, with relatives and friends coming from far and wide, as well as staff and workers from the estate. The obituaries to "The Little Lady with a Large Heart" were fulsome in their praise of all the active support Helen had given to good causes, and said she was noted for her work on many charities, including the various Ogilvie charities, and was greatly loved by all who knew her. Miss Nellie Webster, the Aldringham school-teacher, never forgot her. In 1977, at the age of ninety-one, she spoke of "Mr Stuart's wonderful little wife" with affection. "She took such an interest in the School," she said "and always wanted to hear the children sing when she came. She was a real friend to me. A real friend. I could really talk to her. She was so kind, and used to send the car for me to go to tea with her. When she died, I couldn't get over it. I felt one of the family had gone. I cried and cried. She was such a sweet person. A real friend." This was the feeling of all who knew her.

Stuart was desolate. The idea of living at Sizewell alone - without his beloved little wife and loyal companion of forty-four years - was unbearable. Sholto stayed for a few days, and suggested Stuart went abroad for a month. He needed a complete break before returning to his work. Stuart agreed to go.

Upon going back to the office on April 3rd, Stuart wrote to the Managing Director in "the Book" (as it became known) "I wish upon my return from my prolonged absence abroad to express my extreme satisfaction with the conduct and progress of work carried out under your sole management during my absence. The present state of affairs encourages me to look forward to a season of ever-expanding prosperity and the commencement of a new year in the development of Thorpeness." He then plunged into details with regard to taking over an unexpired lease for the Coastguards buildings. What would be the cost of converting the four Coastguards cottages as per the plans he left and the additions to the larger fifth house? No item was too small for his notice: why had certain concrete gateposts not been delivered? (Answer: Because the iron hooks for hanging the gates

on had not yet arrived) He hoped Goodwin had not neglected soaking thoroughly the freshly-planted birch trees ... the pine screen should also be watched ... they would also pay for a good watering ... take it from the tank not straight from the (cold) well... "I hope the palms have not been allowed to go dust dry ... N.B. Please remind me about the end of this month about transplanting (1) Barrie's Walk Phormiums; (2) The new Cypresses Macrocarpa to be obtained from Notcutts. I was very pleased with the general neatness of our garden village on my return from abroad. *Picnicking on the Golf Course.* I observed this abominable practice was again commencing despite our clear notice ..."

It was clear that G. Stuart Ogilvie was again getting into his stride. He sat up far into the night planning his new prestigious Golf Club House at the end of Lakeside Avenue. He called for estimates, the cost of road-making here and elsewhere, progress costs on the Laundry, Beach Farm Dairy, and other buildings in hand or in contemplation. He rowed round the Meare, inspected all the banks, complained of features damaged or missing. Where was the cannon? The latch on the Ladies' Lavatory was broken. The Dragon's wing was bent flat. The Crocodile was in a sad state of dilapidation. None of the fantasies had been repaired or repainted. Why was this not reported to the Managing Director in the Book? (Answer: The work was scheduled for next month).

Every detail in every department he looked into personally and wrote about copiously in the Book. On one item, Mr Wilson had obviously not agreed with a request Stuart had made. Stuart replied "I desire the Manager to exercise his full authority on all executive matters but where - as is bound to happen sometimes - the creative policy of Thorpeness overlaps or impinges ... I am sure I shall receive the loyal co-operation of the Executive in carrying out my wishes even if the Manager may have strong personal views

verbally explained his views to me since my complaint but *there is no record here.* If later I have to refer to this matter to refresh my memory ... I accept the Manager's views - the point is *if these views are not recorded* the Book on this information is *useless to me.*"

Sholto came down frequently for the night. The staff were always delighted to see him. The butler, Mr Roberry, Roberta the cook and Bertha the head housemaid (who had also been Helen's personal maid), were all carrying on their work with their understaff as before, but they missed their Mistress dreadfully. The house had always run like clockwork, but under the friendly guidance of one head. "Now" (as Bertha confided to Sholto) "we have no-one, as the Master doesn't understand - he just knows how he likes things." She could speak her mind with Sholto, because she had been the children's maid at Woodbridge Lodge when they were young and many a time had to keep him in order.

In spite of occupying himself fully with his work, Stuart said how lonely he was in the big empty house - particularly in the evenings at dinner, eating alone, sitting alone. Sholto said "You need a housekeeper - a lady companion housekeeper." "What an appalling idea!" Stuart exclaimed, "Having to make conversation night after night to some silly woman!" "Think it over", Sholto suggested.

Stuart continued to work feverishly, obsessively - trying to fill the void. The Country Club opened for a week at Easter which, with the weather good, proved most successful. The improvements to amenities,

as to the wisdom of my action ... he is relieved of the responsibility in the results, however disastrous or otherwise. I trust that such clashes of opinion will be very rare ..." They did not occur too often, but discrepancies on jobs done - or not done - were quickly picked up. Why had the hanging baskets not been returned to the Hall for refilling? Stuart wanted an estimate for some afforestation and was told 'Not in the Budget'. "Nor did I expect it" he wrote tersely, "but I have mentioned the necessity". Another time he wrote "The Records and Replies in this Book have been most unsatisfactory ..." (and explained what the Book was for). The Manager had not written the answer to his question. It was no good saying "... but I *told* you ..." Stuart stated. "The Manager has including new furniture in the public rooms, were applauded. The dance to a band ("The Follies" from Ipswich) was well attended. The new garages, Shell Petrol Pump and repair and accessories depot at Beach Farm were also much appreciated. The Suffolk County Golf Union held an Open Meeting the Club would be managed on truly democratic lines by a committee of workmen. It would be a comfortable shelter where those from a distance could take their midday meal, and would provide a pleasant rendez-vous during leisure hours. He went on to list the activities which would take

The opening of the Workmen's Club in 1928

at Thorpeness, and the Links were acclaimed to be in first class condition. Everything seemed to be going well, but to Stuart the loss of Helen was unbearable. The pain and hollow emptiness would not go away. He took the weekend off and went to visit Sholto in Surrey. Despite Stuart's reluctance to entertain the idea, they discussed looking into - without commitment - the possibility of engaging a companion housekeeper.

The next big event was the opening by Lord Huntingfield on July 3rd 1926 of the new Hall and Workmen's Club. Some 250 people attended, the Leiston Observer reported. Mr Ogilvie thanked Lord Huntingfield for coming and explained that place there (including whist and dances so the ladies were not forgotten) and also the sports on the cricket and recreation ground. For one penny people could even have a hot bath if they so wished! Nor had the needs of the more serious-minded been neglected. The cosy reading and writing room where the daily papers were provided already had an extensive library. There was also the large stage, admirably adapted for dramatic performance - the proscenium being opened up by folding-doors (modesty prevented him from naming the inventor!) He praised his own loyal workforce and, like Lord Huntingfield, deplored the strike after strike in the country, bringing lost trade, misery and loss of work - often brought about against the wishes of a large majority of the people. "The cruel and crying evils can never be cured" continued Mr Ogilvie "until the liberty of every member of every trade union is assured by secret ballot, so that each man can record, without fear or favour". Finally, in a burst of rhetoric, he pleaded for "goodwill among all men - without which this village, this beautiful hall, would never have been built. It is by love alone, love of King and Country, of Good and God, that the soul of our great people can attain unity and strength - and survive."

It was shortly after this that a Mrs Pearson arrived at Sizewell as a Lady Companion Housekeeper. She was the widow of a clergyman, in her sixties. Sholto had been asked to go to an agency and vet some likely applicants. Stuart then went up to interview a short list of three. The result was Mrs Pearson arrived, somewhat flustered but eager to please. Stuart was confident she would soon learn how the house was run, and asked the staff for their assistance. "It was a good idea," he told Sholto, and he obviously

found her flattering solicitude for his welfare and all that he did or said, an agreeable change from silent loneliness.

Thorpeness was packed out and the Season going well. They had managed to get an advance from the Ipswich Building Society of first £1,000 and then £1,200 for building Greyfriars in North End Avenue and Barn Hall opposite the Meare. Also, for £750 Blake & Sons were laying piped water, with engine and pump from the Meare, to seventeen of the golf greens. A Mr C. B. Bow had been engaged as Company Secretary from November to take the burden off Graeme Kemp who had asked to be relieved of this duty in view of the increased work he now had as Works Manager. He had held the post since 1911, and was warmly thanked for his valuable services. His salary was to remain as for the two posts.

The Regatta went off with its usual excitement, and Christine, Stuart's daughter (now divorced from Capt. Young and married to a Mr Alec Alcock) gave away the prizes. Hanna, Alec's widow, had also remarried, and was Mrs Herbert Culver, living in

Sailing on the Meare in the 1920s

Weybridge. Stuart's family and grand-children were down at Cliff House and the annexe for their summer holidays with Sholto's household, and Mrs Pearson went out of her way at the Hall to be ingratiating - gushingly so. The children were told to come over and play in the grounds and invite friends to tea and tennis parties there. On the face of it, all should have been well. Unfortunately, the children could not stand her ...

Sholto always treated his two elder children, Glen and Ailsa, in a very adult way. He often asked their views or opinion on matters. One day in September, while watching some tennis, he said "Mrs Pearson seems a very pleasant person, don't you think?" "No!" they both almost shouted. "But," he said "she's very nice to everyone and does everything she can to make you all happy." The subject was dropped, but they could see that their father, too, had his doubts. Three months later, at the beginning of the Christmas holidays, they were shocked when Sholto announced to them that "Grandad and Mrs Pearson are going to get married." Gladys tried to explain that it was difficult for Grandad, living in the same house. Mrs Pearson could not be a proper hostess, and she could not go about with him very well, not being his wife. It would make things easier for him. Sholto looked far from happy. Stuart and Mrs Pearson were married quietly in Aldringham Church at the end of January 1927, and went on a two months' holiday in Jamaica. No Photographs were taken.

When he returned at the end of March, Stuart was obviously in a much more relaxed state. He recorded in the Book his extreme satisfaction at the progress of all development work carried out during his absence. It reflected the greatest credit to the Managing Director, the Works Manager and the entire staff. The next weeks went on with details on every aspect of work in hand - the extensive alterations to the renamed Dolphin Inn (which was not to be called a hotel), the

golf course, the cricket ground, buildings in hand, and, of course, the gardens.

The idea of a prestigious hotel was still one of his dreams. To be called "The Castle Hotel", it would have 268 beds for guests, 20 for their servants, and 75 for staff. The estimated cost was £120,000 (£90,000 for building and £30,000 for furnishing). Sadly, he had to write to the architect, W. G. Wilson, in London: "For financial reasons I have had to abandon my fifteen-year-old conception of a central hotel over cloistered shops ... I therefore propose to erect a very similar building to contain twenty flats ... to be called Possada Mansions ... I have already devoted over a hundred hours of concentrated labour upon this Master Building." He then gave details of elevation, thickness and types of walls, central heating, with open fireplaces in the drawing rooms, even kitchens with rubbish shoots to removable bins, and innumerable picturesque features. Alas, it was never to be built. Instead, in 1936, architects completely altered and amended the plans and built - on a different site - The Headlands.

Meanwhile, other matters pressed. The River Hundred upstream was not being kept cleared; there was constant consultation with regard to going onto main drainage; Mrs Mason in the House in the Clouds urgently wanted a ground floor extension as a 'bear garden' for her lively family and friends. The improved Dolphin Inn opened at a rush weekend. It was chaos. The kitchen premises were too small and the passages too narrow. The manager could not control the staff who were falling over each other serving drinks in the lounge or food in the dining-room. The cook gave notice - but was persuaded to return to her post (or stove!) Stuart received a detailed report, blaming his design. Typically, he thanked the Managing Director for his frank criticism and took the responsibility, but pointed out that both the Managing Director and the architect Forbes Glennie had vetted these plans and not

The improved Dolphin Inn

criticised them. It was difficult getting a quart into a pint pot, but changes would be made. These problems were subsequently resolved.

It always worried Stuart if a man had to be laid off. A chit to Graeme Kemp on May 17th 1927 said "Could you find work for one of my gardeners, Balderston, whom I've had to get rid of simply because the younger gardeners require higher wages". Graeme replied that far from requiring more labour, they would have to reduce it. After searching around Stuart was later able to write that he had found Balderston a job at a better wage. Stuart also suggested they should employ an old retired shepherd, Mr Chilvers, from The Follies, Aldringham, to patrol the common and golf course from 12 noon for £1 a week, to see that picnickers and visitors kept off the course and used only paths. Stuart pointed out Chilvers did not have to walk about all day but could sit at various vantage points and stay at home if the weather was wet. He would be paid just the same.

Stuart often showed sympathy for the old - possibly because he was increasingly aware of his own age. His impatience with his managers or directors urging prudence when he wished to rush forward and make sure that he saw his 'dream' finished, became more and more apparent. What he needed was ready cash; more advances from the Bank; more loans. He had been assured by a Mr B. McCullom, a long lease tenant of Drake House, that he could obtain a loan of £50,000 for Thorpeness to build a small house on 'Look-Out' site beside him, but this failed - ostensibly because of fear of coastal erosion. Stuart was bitterly disappointed. "This means the development of Thorpeness will be arrested just as the tide begins to run strongly in our favour. Unless a financial accommodation is forthcoming, I cannot expect to live to see the materialisation of my dreams ..."

Again, perhaps to relieve his stress, or to make sure his village was not going to be ruined by shoddy workmanship or lack of attention to detail, the Book showed that Stuart's searching eye was everywhere. "There is a finger missing off the Birdcage Walk statue. Why was this not reported?" Repair done. There was a bramble smothering a rose in the Rose Arch ... A dying birch should have been cut down to 18 inches off the ground ... then there were the Country

to the architect. He had just completed more standard houses for a portfolio to be offered to prospective purchasers of leases. "G.K. has been of much assistance in advising upon constructional details. I have chiefly devoted myself to plans suitable for Lakeside and North End sites" he wrote "at prices ranging from £1,372 to £2,610, the latter being particularly picturesque and commodious ...

The Meare in 1929 showing Lakeside

Club curtains ... (Stuart's chauffeur's wife, Mrs Edworthy (an excellent seamstress) would make them more cheaply). The Country Club wall ... had Graeme Kemp the labour to finish it ? And how much would it cost ? (Answer: "£60. Yes, labour available but money is not, though. We have *overspent*.") "Oh dear! Oh dear!" wrote Stuart.

He was still doing the overall design of Thorpeness houses before handing them over

I have added another 'golf' or 'dormy' bungalow at the low price of £746!!"

The money situation was becoming desperate. The Manager, Roy Wilson, suggested they should sell The Dolphin. Stuart consulted Sholto, who thought that to get a better price the plans for the extension should first be completed, and then they should offer the entire hotel and its goodwill, furnished or unfurnished, to the L.N.E.R. Sholto could arrange an interview with their

General Manager. Sholto also arranged to contact Lord Bethell of Barclays Bank, Fenchurch Street, as to the best method of raising the proposed loan upon Thorpeness property. This resulted in Stuart receiving a questionnaire to answer on the drainage system, the number of properties, their values, the amount of loans, ground rents and the balance sheet. Stuart furnished all that was required, and, as usual, was optimistic.

Meanwhile, he once again plunged into details. "Commons Patrol", he wrote. "Report fully Chilver's experience during Whit weekend. (N.B. I trod a measure with a young Hebrew and an elderly Bolshevist about a picnic on the Links. I trust Chilvers had no further trouble with them)" Answer: No trouble. Several people were asked to leave. One car load actually took out a methylated spirit stove to commence operations. Stuart had a number of good Jewish friends, mostly in London and in the Arts or Law. Some used to come to stay at the Hall, but there was still quite a strong anti-Semitic feeling in Britain at that time. Most London clubs and golf clubs did not admit Jews. The question then arose at Thorpeness Golf Club. What should they do, they asked Stuart, if someone Jewish wanted to join? As the Club was run by the members and applicants had to be proposed and seconded, Stuart recommended that each one be judged on merit, but care should be taken that they did not then swamp the place with their friends, as it was alleged was happening at Frinton and some other resorts. As for Bolshevists, the fear of the communists turning militant and emulating the pogroms of the Russian Revolution was much in the forefront of politics at the time.

The second Mrs Ogilvie evinced the desire to become a Director of Thorpeness Ltd, so that she could join in discussions, and help. She was voted on, and in June a note recorded that "Mrs Ogilvie and I were delighted with the tone of the re-dipped chairs in the Country Club." (These were the Lloyd Loom ones chosen by Stuart's daughter Christine a cheerful blue, now brown). Mrs Ogilvie liked 'presiding' and giving the prizes at functions, and was not at all pleased that Lady Jackson was presenting the prizes at the Children's Regatta that year. She did not attend that event. Stuart was pleased for her to take on responsibilities and to run the house - although this had not always gone well and some of the old staff had left. New young faces seemed to come and go, he noticed. Post-war maids were 'difficult and tiresome' though, he was told by his wife. She had offered to take over the secretaryship of the Primrose League, which was appreciated by the Committee. Miss Flick, however, was to be Assistant Secretary, and do the day-to-day work.

Stuart was glad his wife was busy. He had enough on his plate with buildings in hand and the ever-present financial problems. The loans he had hoped for failed to materialise. The Season was going well but it was constantly impressed upon him that some drastic changes would have to be made. At the end of the year it had been decided at a Directors' Meeting to proceed to erect a power house and install electric gear at a cost of £2,130, but that the Almshouses and Workmen's Club Charity would contribute £400 and £485 towards the installation of their electricity supply, and thereafter pay Thorpeness Ltd five pence per unit. They had also sold on long lease house sites, and were to build the houses for their clients in North End and Lakeside Avenues. To speed up the next phase of building, the Board decided to engage Mr Forbes Glennie as the Company's architect full-time at a salary of £200, plus the use of a house.

The meeting was a lengthy one. The Chairman concluded by reporting that Mrs Ogilvie had resigned her seat on the Board owing to the increased demand on her services in other directions. In actual fact, she had not attended a single meeting in 1927.

Chapter Seven

New Brooms and Drama

STUART entered the year 1928 in more optimistic spirits than he had been in for some time. He had planned 1928-29 as a phase of intensive development. His plans for West Bar, the new water tower and the street of most attractive houses (all designed for winter as well as summer habitation) and his portfolio of several designs for leaseholders, were now completed. Forbes Glennie had moved to Thorpeness and was pushing on the projects. The Managing Director strongly urged prudence and a slow approach. Stuart thanked him for his concern but said he was too old for prudence and going slowly and he took full responsibility for proceeding with the utmost urgency. It was work for his building force, and the sooner the buildings were up the sooner they would bring a return. After this clash of personalities and mutual lack of confidence, perhaps it was no surprise when, on the 14th March, Stuart received a letter from Mr Wilson resigning his position as Managing Director and General Manager of the Company as from 17th March. This Stuart accepted, and at a Directors' Meeting on the 19th it was resolved that Mr Wilson be paid his salary plus a present of one month's pay with the use of his house "The Ness", Lakeside Avenue, until the end of the month, when it would be required.

A Commander C. H. B. Foxley was engaged as Wilson's successor, and the 50 ordinary shares transferred to him. Needless to say, as with all 'new brooms' a number of changes were made, and ways and means were sought to be more cost-effective. The Manager proposed to dispense with a permanent secretary at the Golf Club and only to have a temporary one from July to September. The Country Club would be run by a Manageress. Bookings for the Club and The Dolphin would be made through Head Office where Miss Lewis, previously in charge of bungalows, would be promoted to Secretary to the Manager. Another woman would be taken on to look after the bungalow or house bookings and clients' needs. Efforts would be made to get the local authority to take over some of the Thorpeness roads; also the kerbing of these should be continued with standard concrete kerb stones supplied by Thorpeness Ltd. Houses likely to be used in the winter were to be wired for electricity as a first priority. There were adjustments in future contracts on properties.

The budget for 1928-29 was carefully set, and the important item of 'ways and means' approved, with some alterations to past plans. Stuart continued to keep his eye on every detail and make comments in the Book, be it the gate with a broken latch swinging in the wind or a gardener watering in the heat of the day instead of the early morning or evening. Stuart wanted to buy hurdles made in the Lord Robert's Workshops, but was told they were double the price of the hazel ones they used. "I am sorry, we clearly cannot afford them", he wrote, "I should have liked to help the blind ex-soldiers."

The Season, as usual, went with a tremendous swing, all houses and the Club packed out with people bent on making the most of their holiday. Most people came for a month, while leaseholders were usually in residence for the whole of the school

Some of the attractions on the Meare:

Top left: "Wendy's House"
Top right: "The Pirate's Lair"
Bottom: "Peggotty's House"

holidays. Golf matches (for a number of trophies), the weekly tennis tournaments and the Annual Open Tennis Tournament (which attracted a large entry) were now regular features, while the Children's Regatta and fireworks never failed to get crowds of people and wide publicity.

As usual, at the end of the Season, every aspect of the Company was scrutinised and assessed. The weekly receipts from the Golf Club (green fees and buffet), The Dolphin (hotel and bar), the Country Club and the Meare, were studied and compared with previous years. All were very considerably up. Likewise, there were over 300 entries for the Regatta as opposed to 200 the previous year.

The boat-house had looked splendid at night, picked out for the first time with electricity. Stuart wrote in the Book "Most satisfactory" and felt moved to add "A Note: I sat for awhile watching the merry and multi-coloured crowd that filled the boat-house, Barrie's Walk, the Bay Reserve and the gardens bordering upon the silver Meare, where innumerable boats flitted to and fro. The Old Mill and the hooded water tower lifted and peeked above the trees and roofs of the gaily decorated houses which fringed the lake. The blue horizon was laced with woodland greenery - a scene of innocent happiness and infinite beauty. Forbes Glennie and Graeme Kemp - to whom this note is addressed - above all of my loyal staff, were with me in those days seventeen years ago. I wonder whether they, too, recalled as I did the ugliness and stark desolation of this treeless, waterless uninhabited spot when we began our work. It is good sometimes to remember and offer up a silent thanksgiving for, in truth, a great endeavour has been singularly blessed".

Already over sixty Club bookings had been accepted for next year: some ladies had been practically quarrelling over wanting the same rooms. They had been told that no guarantee could be made that specific rooms could be reserved for next year. They were also warned that tariffs might possibly have to be raised for next August, particularly for the bed-sitting rooms. "V.G." wrote Stuart. There was, of course, always the question of the overdraft. This did not go down. And with the added expense of having to increase the water and electricity supply and the sewerage problem for the growing village, new loans would have to be found from somewhere. There was also the vexed question of accommodating the extra staff required in the summer (approximately thirty people) without taking paying room-space from The Dolphin, the Club or the Guest House. The idea of building dormy houses for ten men and the eighteen women was being bandied about - but it was all money ...

Stuart came face to face with the servant problem just before the end of the Season. On September 11th he wrote "I beg to report the following incident which occurred last night. I was about to retire at 11.20 p.m. when Mrs Ogilvie appeared in her dressing-gown and reported that the servants (who had all gone to bed) had been rung by three excited persons who demanded to see me, stating they had come from the Country Club. I said I would see them in my study. They proved to be Grace Gibson and Lily Taylor (coffee-room maids) and Harold Holly (who described himself as 'Veg. Cook'). The girls were at first very excited. I informed them I was not accustomed to listen to complaints at 11.30 p.m. but as they were apparently leaving Thorpeness tomorrow morning I would hear what they had to say, and promised that justice would be done to all. I then proceeded to take notes. As usual in these cases it was difficult to gather the truth

from the flood of irrelevant and incoherent complaints poured forth. The matter seemed to resolve itself with the wage, less five shillings deducted from breakages in the kitchen for which they denied all responsibility. They had never been informed when they were engaged that such deduction would be made. Gibson made the curious statement that crockery was broken in the kitchen "on purpose". When I questioned her on this point she was somewhat vague, but I gathered that plates were sometimes deliberately knocked off the table or thrown from one servant to the other in a 'catch-who-can-catch' parlour pastime in which these maids did not participate.

The second cause for dissatisfaction was that the members' tips this year were far below those given last year, and that the hours in the lounge and on dance nights were very long and arduous with no corresponding recompense in tips. At times the girls did not get to bed till 3 a.m. They attributed the shortage of tips to the members' general dissatisfaction with the food and kitchen arrangements, which, owing to the perpetual change of cooks, were very bad. (I elicited from the maids that they had received £13 each in tips in about seven weeks). They made certain other representations about the Management which I did not go into. The 'Veg. Cook' maintained a gloomy silence in the background. I gather he had been fined ten shillings for breakages, and adversely criticised the procession of cooks and consequent confusion in the kitchen. He was glad to hear the rumour that last year's chef was to be engaged next Season.

During the twenty minutes session of this impromptu court, the two girls recovered their equanimity - having caused one of my servants to re-dress and wait up to let them out - thanking me most respectfully for having listened to their grievances. I promised that the whole matter would be referred to the Manager, Commander Foxley, and carefully considered and strict justice observed. (Gibson dryly remarked I should hear another story from Mrs Green and I replied that that was quite likely). I should be glad if the Manager would go fully into these cases and report thereon. I am sure he will conduct the enquiry in a strictly judicial spirit."

The Manager replied at length about the endless trouble he had had with girls and the kitchen staff, their lack of care, and wastage. At no time had the girls been later than 12.45 a.m. - and this only on rare occasions as only two were left after midnight in order to clear away glasses. He had in fact frequently asked others to leave after the dinner shift, and not hang about the dance-floor tittering as they watched the dancing. It was a pity the first cook engaged (sent by the Café Royale) was a drunkard. "In conclusion," he wrote, "I am only too sorry that the Chairman has been worried at such a late hour by these stupid and miserable servants, and I trust the great privilege he afforded giving them a private interview will not again be extended to any servant on this estate."

On replying, Stuart wondered "how far this state of mutiny is due to the perpetual change of cooks ... or to having a woman Manageress ... the Manager must determine ..." and added "One further comment must be made: I have frequently noticed that in his loyal desire to shield me from unnecessary anxiety the Manager sometimes keeps disturbing facts like the above from the knowledge of the Book. I trust he will not do so in the future." The matter had been resolved fairly but a number of changes were decided for the next year. Stuart was not very happy either about the way the accounts were presented each month, and queried a number of points. He was delighted, however, when for the first time in seventeen years at the instigation of this new Manager there was produced a detailed agenda in advance for 1929 with a carefully compiled list of prospective developments, together with 'ways and means' of the financial requirements. Much correspondence followed on ways of making savings on many and varied topics.

Stuart continued to be concerned over details of the gardens and plantings, and also urged the Manager to watch 'errors of taste' creeping in, such as the brown oak post put adjacent to the black-tarred finish of a house. He also ordered suitable pictures, sporting prints and the like, to be bought for The Dolphin to give it more character.

He felt the year's progress had been encouraging, and he was lavish in his praise of Commander Foxley's management, and his staff. The usual end of Season bonus

The Dolphin Inn

63

Westgate Bar from the Country Club

awards and events took place, and then the busy programme of maintenance, road and sea-defence mending and building began. The main projects were the staff dormy houses he had designed, and the new West Bar Water Tower with its two houses integrally attached.

The second Mrs Ogilvie had kept herself occupied with a few charitable works and meetings of the Primrose League. In December she opened the Church Bazaar in Leiston, and said she was "not keen on coming forward on these occasions but the present one was such that deserved her heartiest support." She took her text as "Zeal and Enthusiasm" and emphasised these points. Such sentiments would not have surprised Stuart when he read the report in the Leiston Observer because - as he had dolefully confessed to Sholto - her "zeal and enthusiasm" was driving him mad. He had

married a religious maniac! Furthermore, she was perpetually trying to 'convert' him. It was 'his duty' to go with her to church (which he certainly had no intention of doing), added to which she nagged him incessantly and was at her worst when he was suffering from an attack of gout. It was God's will. He should give up his port - and his claret. Then it was unnecessary to have these full-course dinners every night when they were alone ...

"I shall eat what I like and I shall drink what I like!" he had roared. Now he noticed his excellent dinners at night were deteriorating. He complained. He sent for the cook, but the loyal Roberta Meadows was quite upset and said she was following orders. The household staff were not happy. Some had left. Stuart took this up with the second Mrs O. who said she would see what she could do but "they were so difficult".

"Oh, Sholly! What have I done!" he cried. "I should never have married her! There's no fool like an old fool!"

In the evenings, meanwhile, over the past few months he had been taking his mind off the harsh realities of life with a brilliant idea. Like his friend J. M. Barrie whose children's play 'Peter Pan' was making a fortune in royalties for the Great Ormond Street Children's Hospital, Stuart would write a children's play and make the royalties over to Thorpeness. Musicals were all the rage. It would be a musical. He had consulted his musical daughter, Christine, and she had already written several numbers. The draft of the manuscript was now completed, called 'The Meadows of Make-Believe.' It was based on the Meare, with the time-honoured theme of Good and Evil ... 'Frogs' Chorus', 'The Demon's Song', 'Songs of the Sea', a 'lullaby' ... and the requisite fair heroine and brave suitor. Mr and Mrs Glennie, accomplished players on the violin and piano, were invited to lunch to go through the music with Stuart. It was a happy way of ending the year. Stuart's theatrical agent was entrusted with the finished work.

The New Year 1929 turned very foggy, and the fog-horns boomed incessantly. On January 31st the maroons went up as the Union Castle, the 'Garth Castle' (7,715 tons), went aground on Sizewell Banks. Lifeboat and tugs were called, but such was the fog that they could do nothing at all for two days. Then, with the help of six tugs the stricken vessel was finally shifted and refloated on a still misty evening tide.

Among the old salts following the event was Sid Booty from Sizewell Gap, and his friend Weston. Suddenly he saw in the breakers a huge conger eel. Both men plunged in and managed to drag it up the beach. It proved to be the largest ever seen, and caused as much excitement as the rescue! The eel weighed 76lb, was 7ft in length, and 15 inches in girth. They sold it to Mr Testoni, the Leiston fishmonger, who did a roaring trade with it on Saturday evening, cutting it up and frying it. During the day (as the Leiston Observer reported) it was a source of attraction and amusement when exhibited in his window with a large placard announcing 'Caught in Carr Avenue' - referring to the state of the road of the old brickyard, which was mostly under water and which, for a long time, they had been trying to get the Council to take over!

Stuart had been trying to get the Council to take over the Thorpeness roads, too, for some time - including Remembrance Road built by the soldiers. Upkeep was costly and labour-consuming. It was for this purpose that he kept up his Annual Day of Annoyance to Aldeburgh traffic of closing Remembrance Road for one day a year - with due warning to the Press. The other issue for which he wanted assistance was that of coast erosion. The money was so desperately needed for building. The country as a whole was becoming more and more aware of the need to protect the coast, and already special conferences had been called in London by East Coast Members of Parliament to try to address the problem and alleviate the burden.

Lowestoft had had to find £200,000 over the past five years. There was also growing concern over the desecration of the countryside since the War, with jerry-built houses going up in ribbon developments and wherever a developer wished. The Council for the Preservation of Rural England had been formed, and Stuart frequently wrote letters to The Times or wherever a correspondence arose, pointing out it was possible to build houses of architectural merit and (without saying he had anything to do with it) that just such a development with emphasis on beauty was being built at Thorpeness. Following such a correspondence, after an original letter by John Betjeman in The Morning Post (which was then carried on in all the leading London papers) Thorpeness received a considerable boost to its publicity. Several papers and magazines sent journalists or photographers for articles in the spring. Among them was John Betjeman himself.

Due to severe frost and exceptionally cold weather, all building operations had to be held up for three weeks at the end of February and beginning of March. Also due to frost, no concrete slabs could be made, which again slowed up the building of the Sanctuary water tower and the houses on West Bar. Likewise, road-making and the laying of pipes were delayed. Once the weather improved, Stuart asked that the men went on overtime to catch up.

During this period, he was ill at Sizewell. Nevertheless, he had the Book brought to his bedside and continued to write his comments or directions. He became very testy when told that Smythe, the builder of the water tower complex, wanted his contract time extended by three or four weeks because of the bad weather. "I trust the Manager did not agree ... and informed him we would hold him responsible for any delay ..." he wrote. "The important thing is to *frighten* him into further activity." "I fear this house will be in course of erection during our early summer

65

Westgate from Westgate Bar

season..." Commander Foxley answered.

"Does not the Manager perceive that if the completion of the last house (externally at least) is allowed to drag into June, the special photographs which we have arranged and from which we expect such lucrative publicity, will be too late, and that it may even be impossible for the house to be let, even in August?" The Chairman would confer ... early next week. Stuart also worried endlessly on various garden problems (several thousand seedlings, and young trees) and pointed out that the manure 'glory pit' must be made and built up properly in repeating stratas of straw manure (including night-soil) and weed slub from the Meare. Did we need more pigs?

The Manager was more worried at the steady increase in the labour bill. "I should be failing in my duty if I did not point out to the Board that *we cannot afford to engage one extra man* ... this extra labour in a great many cases is engaged in what I might term *unproductive* work, inasmuch as it brings in no immediate revenue..." he wrote, adding "The Chairman is fully alive to the financial position.." Stuart, exasperated, replied on March 8th "The position seems serious but not desperate. I hoped I had made it clear to the Manager that the beauty of Thorpeness depends upon its afforestation and gardinage as much as upon its buildings and lay-out ... if the gardens are not planted now ... the new houses will look out upon a shabby wilderness instead of attractive flowerful closes ... these are essential facts ... and as essential as the chimneys ..."

On March 16th, Stuart returned to the office. He commended the concrete factory on having now, with overtime, got on top of the demand, with comments in the Book of "Splendid!" and "Very wise", and continued "These twenty pages in the Book cover a period of five weeks ... when the Chairman was absent owing to ill health from the Company's business ... the irretrievable loss of three precious weeks owing to abnormal weather ... will call for the greatest energy, coupled with perfect organisation, to plant and complete the many new gardens ... and the many replacements in the afforestation department ... under the personal direction of the Chairman. The chit on 'Building Operations' is one of the weakest and most unsatisfactory reports ever presented by a Managing Director ... it seems to accept the situation with the complacency of oriental fatalism. The Board will deal with the matter forthwith. Finance is causing the Board considerable anxiety but no alarm. It will be dealt with next week... Last year's trading figures, excluding the Dolphin, forward booking and advance letting at increased rentals, are most satisfactory." The overdraft stood at £12,218 18s. 11d, and the increase of Loan, due to payments to Reade the builder of £500, at £618 16s. 6d. "The Manager's suggestion that the Book should virtually cease to function during Rush Periods is not practical. Crucial problems in the management of Thorpeness Ltd do not cease to arise because it is holiday time.." Stuart concluded.

The many pages over the next weeks certainly showed that problems on all subjects from drainage sumps to the building of the staff dormy houses and the negotiations to obtain a further £11,000 Loan on the Westgate houses from the Ipswich Building Society, grew no less. The buying of suitable and interesting antique or good second-hand furniture, pictures and ornamental vases for these beamed, prestigious rooms also concerned Stuart. Colour schemes and soft furnishing would be left to the artistic Mrs Glennie. The rooms had to look tastefully - if not luxuriously - furnished for the publicity photographer coming to depict this new phase of permanent residents in Thorpeness.

Easter was a great success, and the majority of the old clients came down. The Manager took the opportunity to obtain their reactions on the new, artistic development of Westgate and the water tower. However, he regretted to have to report that "in no single instance did he find *any enthusiasm* amongst our clients ... many deplored the rapid change of our dear little hamlet ... the artistic heart was being destroyed ... when they came to Thorpeness *they did not want to live in a street* ... The Manager pointed out that "any enterprise must cater not for one class of person and tastes but for all classes, provided those persons were desirable ... It could be that some of our old clients would leave and we shall attract a new class. Perhaps this is desirable .."

"Very true" Stuart replied. "If by our clients the Manager refers to our present tenants who require a cheap cottage to spend a month in by the sea, one would hardly expect them to enthuse over an all-the-year-round luxury house, or an attempt to attract a *permanent*, not a *seasonal* population. The unintelligent cant about 'spoiling our dear little hamlet' was quite seriously administered to the Chairman before the row of Haven houses (the first to be built in Thorpeness) had been finished! ... Thorpeness will never fulfil its Destiny till it becomes an all-the-year-round Residential Village." With No.6 sold on long lease and No.3 let, they had made a good start.

Stuart was now very keen to get St Mary's Chapel (or the new St Mary's Church) built. He had the plans from his original sketch and lay-out back from the architect, W. G. Wilson, but - to keep the cost down - without the side aisles. The cost was estimated at £3,000, with the church furniture as £300. The Board decided that it might possibly be able to start building by the autumn of 1930, but definitely not before - with charity money.

"The hope that he will live to see this chapel finished is never absent from the Chairman's mind," Stuart wrote somewhat sadly. Since his illness, he had become even more conscious of his advancing years, and was not helped by the second Mrs O. constantly reminding him that his life was running out, that he should hand over to his executives and repent and go with her to church. If he had his own church, an ecumenical church, a chapel in memory of his dear free-thinking, broad-minded mother who had left money for 'religious assistance' in whatever way the Trustees felt fit, he *would* go. A framed drawing of the church was hung, at his request, in the Country Club in May 1929, so that summer visitors could see what it would be like.

It was shortly after this that, as reported in the Leiston Observer, Mrs G. Stuart Ogilvie had been present at a sale of work for Aldringham Church held by Mrs Stanford on June 22nd at Stone House, Aldringham. She was not to know it, but this was the last function she was to attend in the area.

Stuart had been getting increasingly annoyed at the deplorable standard of cuisine at Sizewell. If there was one thing he really enjoyed and had always been used to, it was a first class dinner at night. He was a gourmet. He knew his food, and was particularly fond of French cooking. He knew Roberta was a first class cook, yet, as he frequently proclaimed, now a third class boarding-house would do better.

One night a favourite dish he had asked for came in. It was tough and inedible. He was tired, and furious. "Unfit for human consumption!" he exploded. "Why can't I get a decent meal in my own house? Send for Roberta!"

The butler despatched a parlour maid and, not for the first time, the anxious Roberta was ushered in. "Why is this dish inedible?" he said angrily. "Is it made of shoe leather? Why can't you cook as you used to?"

Roberta looked round nervously, nearly in tears. "Oh, sir" she said, "I told Madam that this dish needed best fillet of beef but she said I would have to make do. The trouble is, sir, I never get the best joints and cuts nowadays ... I do my best, sir" and she burst into tears.

The second Mrs O. became very flustered. "The butcher is so tiresome" she said. "I have endless trouble with him ... I will go and speak to him again."

"You may go now, Roberta, Stuart said kindly. "I know you're a first class cook. I will now look into this matter personally with the butcher." But Roberta gave in her notice.

In the morning, despite his wife's remonstrances, saying she would go herself, Stuart drove straight to the butcher in Leiston. "You used to do me so well, Mr Catling," he said. "Now your bills have gone up and the meat you send is inedible. What happened to last night's fillet of beef?"

The butcher became more and more uneasy. Stuart was not in a mood for patience. "Well? Did Mrs Ogilvie order a fillet of beef?" he asked testily.

"Yes, sir. Yes, sir, she did," the butcher replied, "but - not to be sent to the Hall."

"Not *what*?" roared Stuart. "Let me see your book."

What the butcher's book revealed was almost beyond belief. Stuart found that from practically the day she entered his house, she had every week been ordering quantities of the choicest meat to be sent to her daughter in Devon. This had increased after they were married, and lately he, and the servants, had less and less. There was the fillet of beef - and he had had stewing steak! There was the best saddle of lamb he had asked for and which he had been told was not available! And so it went on, page after page.

Stuart drove back in a towering rage. He had been deceived. He had been defrauded. He had been tricked. How dare she! He told his chauffeur to wait at the front door. He stormed into the house, found his snivelling wife, and told her to pack and get out of the house immediately. She could go to her daughter's. Her luggage would be sent on. She would be hearing from his solicitor.

He then telephoned Sholto. What was he to do? All the faithful retainers had left - even Bertha - and now nothing would persuade Roberta to stay. He had only Roberry, the butler, left, and young or new faces who seemed to change every week or two. The only blessing was that he had got rid of that appalling woman. The greatest mistake of his life.

Sholto was sympathetic. They would have to get another housekeeper. "This time we'll find a really good one. You must have one, you know." "Oh, God! Must I?" Stuart cried. "Then let her be an honest heathen. And why not witty and jolly? Anything but a pious bloody prude!"

"Yes, yes. I'm sure we'll find someone." Sholto soothed. "Someone quite different. Yes, entirely different."

Stuart himself could not have written a more startling change of scene than the one which followed this melodramatic event.

Chapter Eight

Comedy and Reality

IF STUART was looking for a change to shake off the doleful and depressing atmosphere of the past two years he certainly got it. It might be said that the 'Play' switched from the heavy drama of Sir Henry Irving to the musical comedy of the Palladium. The Hall had seen nothing like it.

Enter the chief character: the new chosen, educated, lady-companion housekeeper - a plump ebullient woman in her mid-fifties. She usually spent her time between Biarritz and London, and dressed accordingly. She loved her food and her drink, smoked incessantly through a long cigarette-holder, laughed uproariously, and called everyone 'Darling' or 'Pet'. Her name was Miss Irene Hutton; her maxim, loudly expressed: "Everyone must be happy. Have a wonderful time!" She was horrified there was no gramophone in the house. Poor Pet, the place was dead! Should she get one? Stuart said certainly, if she wanted one. The most expensive 'His Master's Voice' cabinet model was delivered, plus a heap of the latest records - jazz, musicals, and a few old waltzes, ballads, music hall songs and arias from the operas thrown in for good measure.

"I know a wonderful cook!" she announced, and had her installed. The meals became sumptuous. "We should have a few guests to brighten things up," she suggested. "Your life has been so dreary, you poor dahling man. May I ask a friend or two?"

"Certainly, if you would like to," Stuart agreed.

At the weekend, they arrived. Sholto and Gladys, with their two elder children, were also invited for tea to greet the guests. There

appeared one couple in their forties and two sports cars crammed with 'bright young things' - all Biarritz friends in their twenties and thirties. They were all dressed in the height of fashion, the young men in sports flannels and blazers and the heavily made-up girls (with short bobbed hair and fringes and one with an Eton crop) had skirts above the knees. Most of the girls wore long swinging necklaces and earrings. They, too, smoked incessantly through long cigarette-holders and helped themselves liberally from the silver boxes which were always around as part of the hospitality of the house. Tea had scarcely finished when they spotted the gramophone at the other end of the lounge hall.

"Let's dance!" a bright young girl cried, and in no time they had rolled back the large oriental rug and were furiously doing the Charleston.

Little wonder Stuart was amazed - and, at the same time, rather amused. The guests were already completely at home, laughing and shrieking and larking about as though they owned the place, while Miss Hutton - in a broad hat and voluminous dress with a long floating chiffon scarf at the neck - bustled about administering good cheer.

"Ah! Dahling boy!" she said, flinging an arm around Sholto's Glen (who was exceedingly good-looking), "We are having a flannel dance tonight. You must come! Girls! Mr Ogilvie's grandson Glen is coming to the party tonight!"

"Oh, good!" they cried, and Glen was dragged onto the floor. At just eighteen, he was far from averse to the attention, and was an excellent dancer. As a schoolgirl of not quite sixteen, with unfashionable long hair held back with a slide, his sister Ailsa felt somewhat out of her depth amongst such sophistication. (She was not allowed to have her hair bobbed, in case (ominously) she was taken to be older than she was).

Next day, Sholto's family were all anxious to hear from Glen about the party. It was apparently quite astonishing. They were, it seemed, half-tight when Glen got there and became increasingly noisy as the night progressed. Then a girl's necklace got broken and they all spent some time, with much hilarity, rolling about on the floor picking up the beads.

"And what did your grandfather think of all that?" Sholto asked. But Stuart, apparently, had just looked on in amazement as though sitting in the stalls watching a new musical. Meanwhile, Miss Hutton drifted round like a schooner in full sail, plying everyone with booze and saying "I love parties!" She was having another one next day before the guests departed, and Glen had been invited. He had also been asked to go to one in France, and bemoaned the fact that he had not got an aeroplane of his own to flip over there in (he had got his flying licence when he was just seventeen).

"The continental crowd are a very fast lot," his mother said disapprovingly. "You don't want to get mixed up with them."

Miss Hutton reigned supreme at the Hall. Everything went like clockwork. It was a lavish land of milk and honey. The dishes were largely French. Miss Hutton was friendly with the staff, and life certainly was not dull.

Stuart never quite knew who would be there. Some of her friends he found quite interesting, others were 'an education', if nothing else. He could not take to jazz, and soon would not have it played in the daytime when he was around. He did not approve of ladies drinking spirits or smoking, nor the modern habit of powdering their noses between courses at meals (which his daughter Christine and daughter-in-law Hanna also did) and Miss Hutton certainly put back the gin.

Fortunately, Stuart genuinely had work he wished to get on with, so he spent considerable time in his study. His theatrical agent, unfortunately, could not find a market for his 'Meadows of Make-Believe', which was thought to be too advanced for the average child. He was also doing the plans for further houses. Then there were the everlasting items which appeared daily in the Book - the outing for his indoor staff at the Hall (on two separate days), the need to increase the depth of the wells following the introduction of wash-basins and more bathrooms, and other problems to be dealt with.

This was a time of recession in farming and of crisis in industry. The slump was world-wide, and started in the U.S.A. and Canada. This added financial worry was exacerbated by Stuart's railway shares having fallen heavily and not bringing in the return as previously. Money was tight all round, and though Thorpeness was full, the visitors were not spending as much as usual. The Golf Club revenue had fallen, just when plans were all set for the new Golf Clubhouse in Lakeside Avenue. Ideas were even being bandied about as to whether or not to sell it. As if this were not enough, there was the vexed question of how to deal with the second Mrs O., whose solicitors were becoming very tiresome in demanding large sums of maintenance. Stuart had discussed this with his lawyers and also with Sholto, who was quite firm.

"Don't mess about with annuities" he insisted. "Just pay her off with one large sum and be shot of her for good."

"What sort of sum?" Stuart asked. "And supposing she dies tomorrow?"

"That sort never dies," his son replied. "Pay her a sum she can't resist - say, £10,000. It will be cheaper in the long run."

The whole matter was discussed at length in Sholto's usual caustic and whimsical way over the dinner-table, and the children's opinions sought. "Tough as old boots! Be shot of her!" was their verdict, and this is exactly what happened. £10,000 was the sum, and she snapped at it. It cost Stuart dear, though, as he had to sell shares at a depleted price. The family heard no more of the

In order to boost the Golf Course, they had managed (in September 1929) to persuade the most famous international professional of the day, Archie Compston, to come and play two matches. The event was widely publicised. However, Commander Foxley was quite disgusted at the professional's behaviour when he came. Compston was surly and never smiled. He

Gladys Ogilvie presenting prizes after the Thorpeness Regatta, 1933

second Mrs O. until a great many years later when Sholto spotted her death in The Times. "£10,000 was cheap!" he cried. "It would have cost us more than double!"

The Season went with its usual verve, and Gladys was called upon to present the prizes at the Regatta. Stuart was glad, at last, to be able to invite his own friends down for weekends or visits and to know that they would be looked after and fed as a gentleman's guests should be. He made it clear, though, that no other guests were to be invited at the same time.

kept his gallery waiting three quarters of an hour on Saturday and an hour and a half on Sunday. The Manager wrote in the Book "He is the most objectionable professional I have ever met and did not attempt to produce anything like his form on either day ... We prepared for him at The Dolphin but he elected to stay with his friend Mr Wagstaff who owns Haven House. However, the very fact that he has played on our course is bound to attract considerable attention to us."

As September proceeded, Stuart asked that an £800 loan he had made be repaid.

On the fourth green of Thorpeness Golf Club in 1930

This was done. He also expressed the sentiments of the Board when he professed extreme satisfaction at the general tidiness and freedom from litter which had marked the village throughout the Season. The usual 'post mortem' took place when the Season was over. July was a loss. The Manager felt this was due to the General Election and the return to power of the Labour Government. Fortunately, August and September were good. The financial position was not altogether happy, though nevertheless there was planned a long list of maintenance and new developments. The new Golf Clubhouse being built was going to be financed as far as possible by debenture shares sold to members. Stuart said he would make up any shortfall privately with his own unsecured loan, to avoid increasing the overdraft at the Bank. His chief concern was now preparing his detailed plans for the luxurious permanent houses for long lease.

The Company was greatly pleased by the publicity photographs taken of Westgate and the water tower. The 'Ideal Home' in its September number gave Thorpeness a four-page, eight-illustrations, feature, stressing that 'beauty and culture' were possible in modern buildings. Other periodicals and papers praised Thorpeness, and showed the picturesque street and olde worlde interiors. The Sunday Express sent a special correspondent down for a long feature article in the more popular vein. "Village built out of Hatred for Modernity - Dance Halls, Cinemas and Promenades banned. Pierrots forbidden on the Beach" ran the multiple headlines. There was a picture of the "Dream Village" looking down Westgate, and another of Stuart. The report carried on at length with the interview and the courtesy received, and how Mr Ogilvie "a tall and almost gaunt figure with piercing dark eyes" had built Thorpeness as a gesture "against the abominable commercialisation of today." He built it for those people who "want to go away for a while from streets filled with super-omnibuses, shouting newsboys, pneumatic picks and glaring electric signs ... Mr Ogilvie spoke with the fervour of a visionary ... of the half a million trees he had planted (and most two or more times because of the sandy soil and climate) ..." This produced an article in the Journal of the Royal Society of Arts referring to "the Paradise at Thorpeness" and that they were "more than grateful to anyone who preserves such a haven of beauty and rest..." Stuart wrote thanking them for their encouragement, adding that "at 72, I clearly cannot expect many more years of useful activity and I am grateful to anyone who can give me the much needed publicity."

The urgency for speed now haunted Stuart. He seemed to have been dogged by obstacles quite beyond his control from the start. First the War, then the aftermath and lack of materials; the world-wide depression, the Labour Government, rising prices, rising labour costs; the everlasting difficulty in raising loans; the short profitable season; the reduction in personal income through the terrible recession in farming, and falling share prices following the New York Stock Market collapse; and now it looked as though he might be cheated out of seeing the fulfilment of his dream through old age - or death.

Meanwhile, all in all 1929 had been a reasonably good year, and although the overdraft stood at nearly £12,000, Stuart found the picture encouraging. In the Book he asked what the dates were for the repayment interest on three different loans he had made. "I may find it necessary to call for this for the upkeep of Sizewell Hall and its household," he added.

January and February 1930 were cold and bleak. Stuart, who seemed to have become more prone to 'flu and heavy chesty colds, was again confined to his bed, from where he studied the future programme of plans and the figures in great detail. As his Manager pointed out unpleasant facts, the outlook appeared to be almost as depressing as the weather. Due to rising costs and labour, the Dépendance (or Dolphin extension) would now cost nearly £2,900. They were spending too much on advertising - was it productive? They must cut down on the gardens and maintenance costs. Forty of the less efficient workmen and artisans would have to be laid off over a number of months: Stuart knew that this would mean many of the older or disabled men who had fought for King and Country. "The Board are fully alive to the financial position which will be discussed next week" he wrote from his sick bed on February 22nd. "They see every reason for the *greatest care* but none for alarm."

The following week Stuart recorded "We are now making an effort to advertise Thorpeness - and more especially The Dolphin Inn - through the medium of our friends and those of Miss Hutton, a very pleasant 'woman of the world.' " He then asked for brochures to be sent to various people and said that a "Mrs Blackwood, a lady with a large circle of wealthy London friends, is staying with us this weekend and thinks she may be of considerable assistance in this propaganda work." This started a series of 'hospitality' visits to Sizewell Hall of 'helpful propagandists', who not only wanted their expenses but a commission on any introductions of theirs who visited The Dolphin. Meanwhile, he admitted after further perusal of the accounts that "the position was more serious than we imagined because of nearly £2,000 deficit on the increased overdraft of £15,000." Though not worried, he thought economies might be made in a reduced staff by switching some men from one type of employment to another "so as to keep all in full employment all the year round". Stuart even offered, if absolutely necessary, a further £5,000 from his very attenuated private capital - if Barclays Bank would not allow a further overdraft by accepting some or all of the Company's ground leases as cover instead of (this time) his own personal guarantee ...

In March, nothing tangible had happened after Mrs Blackwood's enthusiastic visit. However, a number of friends were eager to come and see for themselves this truly unique model seaside resort. It was quite plain that Commander Foxley did not share Stuart's optimism or faith in the smart lady from

London, and said so. Stuart felt moved to write a long memo - which he headed "Quo Vadimus (?)!"

The Manager has on a recent interview with the Board repeated in even more Cassandra-like terms the opinion set forth in his chit. He frankly stated as his opinion that the Board's present financial policy "is a menace to the Company's future! - that the building of West Bar and Westgate was a colossal error; that the erection of the Golf Club-house is very premature; that The Dolphin, when the Dépendance is completed, cannot be made to pay; that the floating debt to the various Building Societies is excessive and that to increase the overdraft at Barclays Bank next year to £20,000 would be extreme folly".

Countered Stuart: "It is obvious that if Mr Bland (the Manager of the Ipswich Branch of Barclays Bank) to whom our Manager will present the Company's 1928 Balance Sheet on Friday next, were to share these unsubstantiated opinions, no future accommodation could be expected from the Bank. The Board, however, wishes to put on record certain countervailing facts, which they particularly desire the Manager to fully digest before his interview with Mr Bland. These facts are:

- That the creation of Thorpeness has, from the first, been a speculation stimulated by imagination but controlled by common sense.
- The Primary Object ... is to ensure the continuance of the Ogilvie family - and more especially of the infant heir, Alexander Stuart, the son of his late eldest son, Alec - at Sizewell Hall ...
- That the wealth of the Company lies, not in its increasing revenue but in the tremendous increment in land values ...
- That by far the greatest of the many dangers which confront the successful development of Thorpeness is the possibility that its creator and controller may be invalided out of service or demise

before the main features of the village, which was determined and recorded some twenty-two years ago, should be sufficiently materialised to enable his trained and clever but totally unimaginative successors to complete his work without making any fatal mistakes.

- The inadequate finance has always been the Board's chief difficulty.
- Trading profits and values of freehold properties have quadrupled within the last ten years - whereas the Bank Loan (even if the proposed further £5,000 be secured) would only have doubled during the last ten years ... The Loans by Building Societies are secured upon certain specified properties and the annual repayment of capital clearly strengthens, not weakens, the Company's financial position.
- The clearly defined development policy of the Board will at the end of this year, viz 31st October 1930, have reached its penultimate stage. No further serious expenditure of building capital (although very desirable) will be absolutely necessary ... and the financial position of our Company should be sounder and easier than at any time during the long, arduous history of our perilously speculative but splendidly successful enterprise.

The Board do not shut their eyes to the fact that we are encountering a period of over-taxation and consequently of severe trade depression," Stuart continued. "The political situation is, moreover, very obscure ... The Manager has been sadly disappointed in his estimated budget receipts up to now in 1930. This may account for his present pessimistic and almost panicky expression of opinions. Our Manager must learn to differentiate between Fact and Opinion ... in this speculative business ... also between Probability and Possibility. The complete collapse of our Company's business is possible but it is not probable. The steady growth of Thorpeness, under difficulties which our Manager would never have faced, has not been due to Fear (which is as contagious as smallpox) but to a keen foresight as to Possibilities.

The Board does not require the Manager to waste his valuable time in replying to this chit but they do wish him to thoroughly digest the above essential Facts before interviewing Mr Bland."

The Manager did reply, with restraint, stating he felt it was his duty to give his opinion.

Stuart's main occupation then became the full lay-out, plans and elevations for cheap but commodious and well-built houses to sell on 75-year leases for less than £1,000, with a ground rent of £12 10s. 0d. He had planned seven to hand over to Forbes Glennie, who had approved them and made some valuable suggestions, and which it was hoped would be ready to include in the portfolio of designs for North End and Lakeside Avenue in time for Easter.

The new Golf Clubhouse was nearing completion, and Stuart was anxiously supervising the "gardinage" to make an attractive setting. Before the end of March, three hundred and four year-old gorse seedlings (not including the gorse hedge already planted), broom, tree lupins, ilices and Scots pines (and sweepings from hay-lofts to seed bare patches, which would also include wild flower seed) were all put in, together with a quickset hedge on the western boundary. Everything was to be finished and perfect for the opening of the Clubhouse by Sir Herbert Hambling on April 30th 1930. Stuart had to approve every detail, even the curtains. The materials he envisaged could not be found. Miss Irene Hutton had been of great help, he said. Samples were sent from the best London shops. Finally, it was the Manager's wife who solved the problem.

The Opening Day dawned. The luncheon for fifty-two local 'notables' and members of the Press all went perfectly. Sir Herbert,

in a lively speech, said they should all be eternally grateful to Mr Ogilvie for building the wonderful Clubhouse and for all the money he had poured in to create the beauty of Thorpeness.

Stuart, having thanked Sir Herbert for doing them the honour of becoming their President, went on to praise his own loyal workforce, many by name.

"Mr Forbes Glennie has been associated with Thorpeness from the beginning of the venture (twenty long years ago)" he said, "and I hope he will still be here to complete our Dream, long after I, the Dreamer, take my well-earned rest in the Ogilvie 'Garden of Sleep'. The sole ambition of every artist is to leave this sordid world of ours the more beautiful for his coming. Thorpeness is an example of this passionate striving after the beautiful ... to recapture and preserve the peace, the restfulness, the infinite charm of English rural beauty which is being so wantonly stamped out under the iron heel of modern commercialism."

The opening of the Clubhouse brought the wide publicity Stuart had hoped it would. It was a leading feature in golfing magazines and local papers, and the London Press Agency was instrumental in general articles describing this unique village appearing in all kind of magazines and papers. They were ecstatic over the Opening of the Clubhouse (yet another amenity), praised the sumptuous six-course lunch, G. Stuart Ogilvie for his vision, and, of course, the Meare. Through the auspices of Sholto, a twelve-page supplement with twenty-five illustrations was written in the British Commercial Gas Association Magazine on "Gas for the Homes of the Future - Thorpeness, a Model Village".

Stuart was delighted to give interviews to the many reporters wishing to see him, and to read articles written by the overseas Press (and not always because they had advertised in them). 'The Civil & Military Gazette' of Lahore, India, had obviously read the lengthy article in the Sunday Express and copied it almost word for word. Others, like the Toronto Star, sent their London correspondent down. "Tudor England revived among the Dunes", "Peter Pan's Land found in Lovely Mere" they wrote. "... planned from the beginning by a master mind ... the burning visionary, G. Stuart Ogilvie ... the chief worry is money ... 'but we are signs on the Meare. 'The Magic Pavilion' and the 'Do not irritate the Brontosaurus' signs were looking shabby ... and why was the crocodile not back in position?

As the summer went on, it was apparent that although Thorpeness, unlike most other resorts, was full to capacity and seemed unaffected by the serious depression which gripped the City and the business world in

The new Golf Club House, 1930

determined not to commercialise this venture' he said. It would have been so easy for him to get the money he needed if they ever fell to the temptations of other seaside town developers". Following all the publicity in the golfing papers, a number of important matches were arranged, including The Suffolk County Union Eighth Championship Meeting to be held in Thorpeness in June the following year. More people also came to The Dolphin to play golf.

Stuart was greatly heartened by the success, and visitors coming so early in the year. He pressed his staff to smarten up the place, renovating or painting the fantasies and general, the people were not spending. The various bars were all taking less, and those people in rented or leased houses were obviously finding money tight. Many (through the Company) sub-let for part of the time. Meanwhile, prices having been fixed before the slump and the many commodities having increased in price, meant that the Country Club, The Dolphin and the Golf Club had lower profit margins. Another point of annoyance being battled with was that the Council had assessed the new Golf Clubhouse for General Rates at £150 whereas Aldeburgh Golf Club (with more accommodation) was assessed at only £80.

Left: "The Magic Pavilion"
(originally a beach hut called
"Rusticana")

Below: "The Dragon's Den"
on Thorpeness Meare

So many people were now flocking into Thorpeness on day-trips that Stuart felt the peace would be ruined. He asked the Great Eastern Railway not to advertise cheap tickets to Thorpeness but to Leiston, as he was in negotiations with Leiston Council that they should take over the running of the beach at Sizewell Gap for their own benefit. They were pleased with the idea of enlarging amenities there.

Stuart also suggested that charabanc excursions should go to Sizewell Gap, for it was being found in Thorpeness that (in spite of twelve more boats having been bought for the Meare), residents could have quite a long wait for a boat if an invasion of the picnicking trippers came in, and they objected to this.

Stuart was becoming increasingly worried about the state of his private finances, and Sholto went down for a weekend. Observing the lavish way in which Sizewell Hall was run under the extravagant hospitality of Miss Hutton, Sholto told Stuart quite frankly that this would have to stop. He suggested that they should go through the accounts together and see where they could cut down. What

they found was staggering. Never had Stuart incurred such bills for wines and spirits, and the butcher and grocers must have made enough to retire on. "Miss Hutton said everything was very expensive now ... Perhaps I should have stopped her entertaining her friends..." Stuart said. "And her trips to London... to interest people in coming here ... did cost a lot ..."

"It must stop," said Sholto. "This is not a free Ritz or a Biarritz Bonanza".

Miss Hutton was called in. The situation was explained to her. Needless to say, she could not understand it. She had done it all for him. She naturally thought he wanted to live like a gentleman should ... She gave in her notice.

With a few conciliatory remarks and regrets, it was accepted. She would leave at the end of the month.

Chapter Nine

The New Era

THE last thing Stuart wanted to face was the problem of a new, unknown housekeeper. The idea appalled him. As if he did not have enough worry without that. It was all such a dreadful gamble. He was thumbing through the Book. Suddenly he stopped. Earlier in June he had written "Miss Cory (a Professional Art Decorator who knows her business) visited Thorpeness." (Actually she was one of the many people entertained at Sizewell in the hope that they would bring in business) "Her report was I think genuinely sincere and enthusiastic. She proposed to make one of a party for a weekend this season". He remembered her. A quiet, sensible, intelligent woman of fifty-five or sixty. He wrote offering her the post. She accepted. He had planned his annual much-needed holiday rest-cure on the continent from July 1st. Now he could look forward, he hoped - with the ebullient Miss Irene Hutton and her entourage out of the way - to coming back to a more peaceful and modest régime in his own house. It would be the start of a new era.

On July 3rd 1930, the Manager, as arranged, carried out the regrettable task of having to reduce the building labour force by eighteen men, first mustering as many men as possible in the Workmen's Club in order to explain to them why this reduction was necessary. He explained the trade recession and that the management had always tried to absorb as much local labour as possible (not always immediately remunerative) but they might have to reduce staff even further if clients failed, trade fell, and they did not receive money to pay the wages. "My remarks were very well received by the men", Foxley wrote in the Book, "and I am of the opinion that if employers of labour would take the trouble to explain to their men why reductions were necessary, there would not be so much ill feeling between the working class and their employers as there is at the moment."

Stuart returned (as he recorded) "from his Happy and Restful Holiday ... as a Giant Refreshed and fit for another year's strenuous and (we hope) capable activity". He congratulated the Manager on the deft way he had handled the labour question. However, he was still worried about the remaining workforce: whether to retain them, or (as advised by his Manager) to dismiss the entire building force other than the key men necessary for running repairs. "How will our Works Manager earn his salary when deprived of building operations?" he asked. "Can we trust our *outside contractors* to build key houses as required at ten pence per cubic foot?"

He felt very strongly that it was his duty to look after, as far as he could, the men on his estate. For instance, when the Manager was told that a labourer with six children had received an eviction order from a condemned cottage, he wrote in the Book "No action was taken as they would have no other house to offer him for three months - and it takes two months for the eviction order to be implemented." Stuart replied "We thoroughly endorse the Manager's action in this matter ... since writing, we have ascertained one of my own cottages to the west of Sizewell Hall will be free almost at once ..."

The spring and early summer had been one of the wettest on record, not only in England but also on the continent. This reflected badly not only on the takings but on the state of the roads. The County Highways still had not decided whether or not they would take over and metal the main road through Thorpeness to Aldeburgh. As August approached, Stuart wrote hopefully "We trust from now forwards the overdraft will rapidly reduce ... and enable the Company to redeem the long overdue unsecured loan from the Chairman who is much embarrassed by the delay in payment." However, August Bank Holiday had the worst recorded weather ever - in the twenty-two years of Thorpeness. Driving rain. Barometer low. No sports at all. No day visitors. A week later, in spite of appalling weather, The Dolphin and new Dépendance were full. Yet why was it that takings were only £8 more than last year? Similarly, the receipts for the Country Club were £349 *less* than 1929. The answer simply confirmed that people were spending less. Bar takings had dropped dramatically, and two doctors at The Dolphin recently were even teetotallers! "Shame! Shame!" wrote Stuart. Holidays were shorter and, as many admitted, they were having to 'tighten their belts' due to the depression.

Stuart was still hopeful that the introductions to the 'wealthy London friends' would materialise. Some were due to stay at Sizewell that month. The Manager was sceptical.

Miss Cory took an active and intelligent interest in the problems of Thorpeness, and was full of suggestions. Stuart always sought the 'woman's point of view', and was glad at last to find someone whose opinion he could respect. The second Mrs O. had nothing to say beyond driving him mad, and the cheerful extravagant Miss Hutton he now saw had been 'there for the ride', having a wonderful time at his expense. Stuart rowed Miss Cory round the Meare, and both he and she noticed a number of details that should receive attention. She was entranced at the Regatta by the fireworks which they watched from the comfort of the lawn at Rudder Grange, which had been most effectively illuminated with thousands of fairy lights. Stuart, however, secretly thought they were commonplace, as might be found at any other seaside resort. He felt that not enough use had been made of the potential scenic opportunities of the background of ghostly foliage in the middle distance of darkling water. This, in fact, was the first fireworks Stuart had attended since little Helen's death when he and Graeme Kemp arranged everything.

The luxury 'key houses' in West Gate had not been sold. Two people who were buying long leases had now cancelled due to the depression. "Woe upon woe," Stuart wrote - in Greek (Euripides) - in the Book. "We are naturally sadly disappointed, but we have no cause to be downhearted. The houses have at least been let." This did not deter him, however, from wanting to push forward the completed plans for the other important buildings in Thorpeness, including the Rotunda. "It may well be that this creation of ours may not materialise during our lifetime but it is our particular desire that full plans, drawings and details of the lay-out of the entire Thorpeness Estate and all its chief architectural features (as visualised by us) should be prepared and filed for future use, as and when they are required, so that when we go, the Manager will be in a position to advise and guide the future Directors of the Company."

The weather improved greatly from the second half of August, and the bookings for September were good. Stuart, therefore, was "very glad to hear that Thorpeness Ltd is at last in a position (without cramping immediate developments) to repay a small portion of the unsecured loans ... advanced by the Chairman" who now found himself in considerable financial difficulties inasmuch as he could not maintain Sizewell Hall, despite having cut expenditure to an irreducible minimum. He had therefore demanded that the minimum sum of £2,300 per annum should be paid to him. Even after a first payment to the Chairman of £800, in September the overdraft was reduced to £11,000. Stuart was delighted.

The end of the Season meant that Stuart's mind turned to afforestation and his beloved gardens - particularly around any new buildings. He was horrified to hear some young saplings had been wilfully damaged. "Can nothing be done?" he wrote. "This wanton cruel vandalism breaks my heart. He eagerly awaited the 'post mortem' on the year and the setting of the Budget for 1931. "Hope deferred maketh the heart sick," he commented.

On October 3rd, the Manager produced his first report and his recommendations. "We are amazed that the brain that can render so perfect a Report ... can during the same week dictate such unintelligent and ill-considered stuff as this," Stuart exclaimed. "This chit shows that the M. has *not yet* apprehended the Board's policy ..." The future cut-backs recommended were particularly in the building programme. Stuart accepted the review of garden staff and estate workers, and had agreed that the concrete factory be closed down and the rails taken up and stored. The Dower House (known previously as The Pavilion) was having heating and lighting put in so it could be let all the year round, at Sholto's suggestion.

The Season had been slightly extended at The Dolphin by the Flat-coated Retriever Association Field Trials, held on Sizewell Settled Estates on October 16th. This was a complete success and they booked again for 1931. Bookings for Christmas and New Year were good. The final Report in December showed an overdraft of over £15,000, but Stuart insisted on paying Christmas Boxes and Bonuses to the staff and workers as usual, and he wrote a special message of thanks and best wishes to them, signed "from a bed of gout". He also approved the purchase at £157 on deferred payment of a Moxon Ford Light Tractor for the Manager - his new toy - to help labour on "my first class Golf Course".

The first three months of 1931 went much as in previous years. New Year was particularly wet but, perhaps because there was little else to do, The Dolphin bar did better than usual. However, several of their "best" clients had not yet paid their bills for August. "I have never known a period when clients were so reluctant to part with their money," Stuart wrote. Fortunately, Mr C. R.. Aldrich had renewed his lease on Sizewell shooting and was making The Dolphin his centre.

By March, the Bank overdraft rose to above the limit of £20,000 due to troublesome demands for rates and income tax. It was no comfort to know that receipts in Aldeburgh and other resorts were also down. The depression was biting universally. "Let us hope for a change in government," Stuart remarked. Easter came and went. Places were full, but takings were down.

Over the past months, Stuart had been working on new designs to be filed for the future. These included 'The Temple Bar Triumphant Arch' on the entrance to Thorpeness from Aldeburgh on Remembrance Road. The Manager pointed out that it would be quite unproductive - simply a memorial. Stuart then changed the name to 'The Fishgate', and planned integral dwellings on each side.

"With traffic streaming through, they would be impossible to let or sell", said the practical Manager. He was asked to file it all the same.

Stuart also felt it wise to turn over all the duplicate plans and sketches he had at the Hall for safe filing at the drawing-office so that they would be available for those coming after him. He was not very happy about his plans for houses on the south bank of 'The Meadows of Make-Believe' - a continuous row of houses beyond Tulip Cot. The trouble was building up a solid foundation and solidifying a treacherous mud bottom. It was while looking at the problems of this marshy area with Forbes Glennie that Stuart became very excited by a new idea. To excavate the boggy areas and build up islands and place one or two artistic and prestigious houses on them. Forbes Glennie suggested it should be called 'Avalon'. The Arthurian connotations set Stuart's imagination working on all sorts of romantic ideas for "an island group with adjoining causeway." He would have liked

to devote the whole of his time and attention to this exciting matter, but he had been seriously indisposed which had thrown him back on his literary work. He had actually for some time been engaged on a philosophical religious work which he called 'Love and Reality.'

In April Stuart wrote "We should be glad to receive repayment of loan due, but *can wait* until our overdraft has been reduced." He could not stop thinking about the idea of Avalon, and in spite of the depression and lack of funds, he asked Forbes Glennie and Graeme Kemp to produce an estimate and cost from his rough plans covering 6,666 square yards. It was pointed out to him that even if thirty-four houses were built (the maximum possible) it was hard to see that it would be cost-productive. Nevertheless, the plans joined the files - along with the Rotunda (a circular group of houses for the west of North End). On May 31st, Stuart also handed over "for safe historic keeping and compiling" his photographic records by Waddell of Leiston of Olde Thorpe and the making of the Meare and other events. Mr Waddell had 200 glass plate negatives of Old Thorpe, and the Manager confirmed that, if still available, he would try and obtain the full set. It was possible, though, that with the shortages during the War some of the plates may have been cleaned to make more photographs.

The overdraft went up to nearly £21,000, but, with debts paid, they could start the Season clear and Stuart was confident the money would soon flow in. He still had not received any more refunds, but he wrote "The Manager has handled the cash situation with great skill."

Whitsun went well. The gardens were looking colourful and beautiful, but the roads, following his own request for economy, were not as Stuart would have liked them.

One of Stuart's friends was Cecil Lay, an architect and poet who lived in Aldringham.

He had created some houses of very original designs in the parish, including the Baptist Chapel on the common and his own house, "Raid's End" (now in 1995 Woodhouse Nursing Home). After lunch at the Hall, he left a number of copies of "Architecture Illustrated" for Forbes Glennie, commenting (Stuart recorded) "It may interest F.G., as it does me, to see the dreadful lack of line, form and beauty in many of the modern buildings - especially when of the concrete type."

Forbes Glennie obviously took this as an opportunity to speak his mind and let off some pent up feelings of frustration. "I cannot but admire those who have the pluck to try, instead of being content to remain copyists all their lives ..." he wrote, "Is his sin greater than that of the architect who reproduces a 16th century building and for his individuality puts a few washbasins inside and lights it with electric light ...?"

Such criticism was nothing new and Stuart took it calmly. He and modern architects rarely agreed - but then he was not an architect. He always said he was a visualiser, an artist creating a picture - a peaceful, beautiful village - a whole stage set - not for the masses but for those who could appreciate it. His two architects, however, were glad to put their names to his designs and to take the credit for it if and when they were acclaimed. "Such is life!" Stuart remarked sardonically.

It is not always remembered that Stuart's passion for landscape gardening and afforestation, often decried as unproductive by his managers, included also the conservation and beautification of the unremunerative areas of the village. The 'sea-walk' or greensward below the cliff, for instance. "We inspected this," he wrote in May, "and were very pleased to see the strong growth of the turf laid there last year. We were pleased to notice that not only various clumps of bent grass were growing freely, but that the sea-pea was gradually establishing itself upon the bare faces of the cliff and on the sea-walk itself. In places the shingle evidently needed further admixture of clay ..." Stuart also planted lupins, tamarisk and similar shrubs along the sandy cliff wherever they would grow, "to give colour to the overall picture" as well as planting gorse on the commons, golf course, and opposite the Whinlands. Rabbits were not the only pests: pine weevils in saplings were also a problem. Stuart personally, with Edworthy his chauffeur, went round removing the maggots as they hatched, and did other labour-consuming jobs, such as tying up rambler roses, to save the head gardener using the small staff on these jobs.

In June, the Manager reported that upon wishing to look back on some early records he had found that these had been destroyed by his predecessor in 1925. This regrettable action had been taken without the knowledge or sanction of the Chairman or Board of Directors, and caused some annoyance.

With less money about, there was an increasing demand for a good class boarding-house. Eventually, Stuart managed to persuade the Manager that it would be a good idea to convert the two westerly Dunes houses, which were less popular as they were not so well-appointed. He submitted his plans, for twenty-five beds. He also remarked that the children in Juvenalia had become 'little pests', bicycling about the grounds and falling into flower-beds. What about transferring to Nos. 3 and 4, The Dunes? They could then convert Juvenalia to luxury bedrooms and bathroom and increase the revenue.

The Manager made tactful 'soundings' among the residents. He found no-one objected to the children. Parents liked to have their children near them, and he pointed out that the bicycle fleet would arrive there daily anyway. The idea was dropped, and the plans joined "the Files." In any event, no major work could be undertaken until 1932.

There was the hope, too, that if their advertising to attract visitors from the dominions and the colonies, home on leave,

The Almshouses in 1926

was to bear fruit, these houses (suitably renovated) might be needed. Special small publicity leaflets were to be got out for abroad, and would be circulated to places as far-flung as Hong Kong, Shanghai, Tokyo, India, Egypt and the Sudan, through their Embassies or Consulates, Banks, State Railways, Travel Agents, Clubs and main shipping agents. Stuart also sought advice as to the best newspapers or periodicals to reach the educated clients he was seeking. No stone must be left unturned in the effort to prolong the Thorpeness Season and to increase the revenue.

Meanwhile, Stuart was still struggling to complete his further plans for a smaller, cheaper type of house for selling on long lease, and for an attractive group of workmen's houses behind the Almshouses to be called 'Rose Walk,' with a trellis of rambler roses along each garden. It did not cheer him to read that the prolonged depression, now commonly referred to as 'The Crisis', had caused holiday resorts all over the country to be doing badly - and that was without endeavouring to maintain a

building programme! However, as August progressed, after the slow beginning of the Season, Thorpeness could report that figures in all departments were up on the previous year and the overdraft was cut to £18,000. "This is just splendid!" Stuart wrote. "It is almost too much to hope that returns can be maintained - if so, by October 31st our financial anxieties will have disappeared."

He had already agreed that, if necessary, he would forego his repayment of loans until October so that, after careful manipulation of payments and funds, they could clear their Bank overdraft and Barclays would renew it on another year's basis. Their publicity effort to attract golfers had paid off, and the Professional Golfers of Suffolk had decided to hold their Championships at Thorpeness.

"This success was entirely due to the Manager," Stuart wrote. "As I know nothing about golf, this department has been entirely in his hands". Then he added "*Note* This does not refer to the Golf Clubhouse, the position of which - and the Plan of which - were designed by the Board before the M. arrived." Stuart could not stand 'vain boasting'. He therefore always referred to plans done by himself as being prepared by the impersonal 'Board'. He then handed them over to his architects to "put the innards in".

Another event Stuart was pleased to announce was that the famous violinist Emilio Colombo (late solo violinist to the Imperial Court of Russia), who, with his charming wife had been staying the weekend with Stuart, had generously offered to give a Grand Concert. This would be held at Thorpeness on Sunday evening, August 23rd, with a collection for charity (being a Sunday, tickets were not allowed to be sold). The charity chosen was the Pearson Fresh Air Fund for Destitute Children. Colombo would come with the well-known cellist, O. Faggotti, his pianist, and five orchestral players, and Miss Megan Thomas, the singer (of wireless fame). They would all have lunch at the Hall (where the Colombos would be staying) while the Manager would arrange accommodation for the others at The Dolphin and would be their host. Full publicity was

being set in hand for this concert, which Stuart confidently hoped would again establish Thorpeness as a place where culture and the arts were catered for.

The great day came. Everything went faultlessly. The hall was packed. Stuart wrote effusively in the Book "... sheer musical delight! ... the enthusiastic appreciation of the full house must have been very gratifying." Then came the blow "...but the financial results were ... disgraceful. The total collection at the hall was £32. This would represent an average subscription of 2/- per head ... yet there were several £1 notes in ... we were ashamed of this paltry sum."

The failure was attributed largely to the amateur ladies who rushed the collection, instead of observing ... and making a personal appeal. The Signora bitterly regretted that she had not held one of the plates. The Manager had thought that after the Chairman's stirring appeal and the splendid performance, donations should have been spontaneous, but he said unfortunately we did not have the

The Hall bedecked with flags of all nations

right type of people in the hall. Apparently, most of the Thorpeness residents were crazy on bridge, and, after a day in the open, they preferred to "settle in their homes to play this dreadful game and do not wish to be disturbed", he said. Furthermore, a glance around the hall showed they appeared to have given their invitation tickets to their servants or children.

Fortunately, the Regatta was an outstanding success. By the end of the month the overdraft was reduced to just over £14,000. "We shall watch the weekly decrease with intense interest," Stuart wrote.

On September 16th, the Country Club closed. The Manager estimated profits would be down by about £400. As other local resorts were reported as going to have a substantial loss, Thorpeness "could count itself lucky to have been so full," as Stuart commented. "Our world is experiencing a universal trade depression unparalleled in the history of mankind" he wrote, "aggravated in England by the criminal extravagance of the Socialist Government which has led the Nation to the verge of bankruptcy ..." He continued at some length, ending "We record these facts for the benefit of those who we hope will read these annals *many years hence...*"

The end-of-year figures were not good. Takings were down. The overdraft was up. "The reason for this," the Manager wrote, "is that there has been a clamour for monies held on account of sub-lets, and this week we have redeemed seven Golf Club Debenture Bonds and interest on all monies invested in that undertaking."

"We quite realise the position and await developments," Stuart replied, and handed over at the same time two more items for the strong-room File.

It was a bitter blow that, after all their efforts, what had seemed good figures could end thus. Sholto again warned Stuart that in these difficult times he was overspending. Stuart conferred with Willett Ram and on October 6th wrote :

"We wish to put on record that after consulting our Solicitor we have once more decided to come to the rescue of the Company by, for the second time in its history, paying off the overdraft at the Bank and advancing £15,000 as a Loan with, if necessary, a further £6,000 as and when required, for floating capital, on the same terms as the previous loan. With all our securities depreciated at the moment, this will involve my letting Sizewell Hall, or at least shutting up most of it.

The Board are now considering what further economies can be effected - including reducing certain staff salaries by 10 per cent" (he then altered this to 5 per cent) "and the dismissal of surplus officers. The Board recognises the causes which have led up to the present crisis, but they also feel that the sole reason for the relatively extremely satisfactory state of the Company's trading account when compared with that of other holiday resorts is entirely due to the amenities and attractions of Thorpeness. This present development of our village could not have been effected without abnormal expenditure, which would not have overburdened the Company in normal years. It is this unique character of Thorpeness which gives us such an advantage over our rival holiday resorts and which leads us to face the difficult future with sober confidence."

Stuart then reminded them that two years ago he had confided in the Manager and the Accountant that he could not, even with the utmost economy, maintain Sizewell Hall unless the Company was in the position to pay him his unsecured loans at a rate of some £2,300 per annum. This being not now possible "has considerably aggravated our present embarrassment" he said, and he had "instructed Mr Ram to take charge of his private affairs re: further financial support of Thorpeness Ltd and he will make the necessary arrangements at the Bank." Chits in the Book on all other details of Thorpeness departments continued as usual: coast erosion and faggotting, selling the pigs, emptying the Meare, "de-furnishing the houses while empty (to effect savings in rates of £104 14s. 3d.)", collection of the Portfolio of key houses built for sale, and other drawings which were kept in the Sales Office, to be listed and placed in the strong-room Files "as they are records and guides to those who will carry on the future development of Thorpeness ... after we are retired or dead."

Surprisingly, the weekly takings went up briefly for two weeks, due to fine weather and trade from the syndicate shooting parties arranged, and over £1,000 was recorded. This did not last, and the outgoings and repayments of debts meant that Mr Ram had to make arrangements with Barclays Bank for the overdraft limit to be raised to £17,000 pending the "re-adjustment of the Company's financial position."

Commander Foxley felt Thorpeness neither could afford him nor needed him. His notice is recorded, but he was willingly working on preparations to plan the best way for the Company's survival over the next six months of winter. "After this week" he wrote, "a new era will be commenced in the finance of this Company. According to decisions arrived at between the Chairman and Mr Ram, the overdraft will now be transferred to a Loan Account and will be closed to us for trading purposes. I have been in touch with Mr Ram on the matter, and I understand that very shortly a credit account will be opened at Barclays Bank, Ipwich, through which the business of the Company will be transacted. That week, therefore, will be a definite landmark in the history of this Company, and it may be that Thorpeness Ltd will never again carry on its financial business through an overdraft - or at least for a considerable time.

I trust the Chairman will not think I am adopting an attitude of superiority but I feel that had he followed my advice many years ago, in which I criticised from time to time in long, considered reports, not only the finance but the *method* we had of dealing with out building profits and monies received from sale of properties, the present unfortunate position would not have arisen."

Stuart would always listen to criticism intently, but did not necessarily agree with it. He replied "We do not consider any useful purpose will be served in discussing past events. We receive the Manager's opinions and prefer to let the facts speak for themselves. We are entirely responsible for the past, present and future policy of the Company. Our private embarrassment is solely due to capital losses during the War and not to monies invested in Thorpeness Ltd, which is perfectly safe."

The Retriever Trials at the beginning of November were a resounding success. The lunch for the thirty-eight people took place in the lounge entrance hall at Sizewell. Miss Cory had arranged for the hot stew and the cold meats to be prepared at the Hall for economy, and Stuart said they would not be supplying cigarettes and cigars this year. A small table was reserved in the window for press photographers and journalists who were covering the event. The day was fine and bright. All arrangements went off admirably and the Manager reported that "he heard nothing but praise and gratitude. The atmosphere was of a friendly house-party, and undoubtedly the valuable propaganda will be of great help to us in our attempt to let Sizewell Hall and some, if not all, of its magnificent shooting."

Sizewell Hall was already in the hands of London estate agents, and Stuart was preparing himself, with some misgivings, to move into the Dower House (after having furnished it with his favourite suitable pieces from the Hall).

He planned to hold a sale of surplus furniture in the spring - unless the house was let furnished, but he still hoped some change of fortune would make moving unnecessary. He was still pinning his faith on a flood of 'colonials' as a result of all their propaganda.

The Dower House about 1910

This was further boosted by a new possibility - South Africa.

A Mr Charles Euan-Smith, who was a friend of Miss Cory's and the nephew of the British Ambassador in Morocco (whom Stuart had known well some years before) volunteered to send propaganda to important quarters in Uganda and Kenya. Stuart was clutching at straws. It was a traumatic time for him, and he sent for Sholto frequently to see that he was doing the right thing.

Stuart loved Sizewell Hall. It was his creation. Perhaps even more, he loved the garden. "It is heart-breaking to think" he remarked to Sholto, as they walked round, "that when I'm gone all this will be lost. It will revert to jungle - but at least there are the trees. The trees will be there."

His other worry was the estate. Farming had been going through its worst long depression for fifty years. As Sholto pointed out, all the farms were running at a loss. They were over-manned, overheads were up, and market prices were down. "Yes," Stuart

agreed sadly. "We shall have to re-organise - but we mustn't sell land. Not the inheritance. With a new Government, times must improve." Meantime, in spite of tactful pressure from the Manager, Thorpeness was still owed well over £1,000 by visitors in December who had not paid for their summer rents. However, Nos. 2 and 3 The Haven were now sold for £1,200 on 99-year leases with ground rents of £12.

The shock and stress of events was having its effect on Stuart. He tired easily and slept badly.

He had always had a strong sense of history. In the distant future, he felt, there would be those who would be interested in looking back on the growth of Thorpeness. He earnestly hoped, too, that those who inherited it would follow his vision. It was, above all, to be a place of restful beauty and peace, a healthy family centre. From the start, therefore, the office had had to keep a Memorabilia Book of photographs, also Cuttings Books and, since 1925, "The Book" itself. He now asked the Manager to ensure that all new photographs had been inserted in the Memorabilia Book. This was done by Graeme Kemp.

Christmas brought fifteen people to stay at The Dolphin, which was encouraging. It was always a jolly affair, run like a country house party, with games, competitions and abundant festive fare. The overall takings were practically identical to 1930. In fact, the overall takings for the Golf Club and Thorpeness as a whole were slightly up. Unfortunately, though, visitors did not stay as long as previously. The village became virtually empty. "We have far too few residents," Stuart remarked sadly. On January 9th 1932 he had, with much regret, to say good-bye to his Manager, Commander Foxley, who had served Thorpeness so loyally. Meantime, Mr Bow, the Company Secretary, would act as Manager until the Company was in a position to make other arrangements. Forbes Glennie, although no longer a salaried employee, was allowed to stay on at 5 Westgate, being paid for his work for each individual assignment.

In mid-January, Stuart was greatly heartened when he came to an agreement with Major Charles Euan-Smith that he would become the next Manager. He was looking for a home in England, having just retired from overseas service. He and his wife inspected Alexandra House (as it was still officially called) and liked it. They were both greatly taken with Thorpeness and the idea of a rent-free house, and an interesting job with remuneration largely in 'perks' appealed to them. They and their small son would have honorary membership of all Clubs, and would be allowed to get all their groceries at wholesale prices at Ye Shoppe (a thing which Stuart never did himself). The Major would also be paid a small salary.

Then the first 'colonial' - a Mr Davis of Hong Kong (a friend of Mr Hitchcock of 9 The Haven) agreed to take a six months tenancy of 6 Lakeside Avenue, furnished, at a rent of £133. "Well done!! Triumph!" Stuart wrote. He was also delighted when advice came that Mr Ram had collected two large accounts owing, and, in all, the current account had been credited with £2,200. "Yes, and we require Debentures issued to us forthwith for this amount," wrote the desperate G.S.O.

The very cold and at times gale force south-east wind and snow of the second week in February were not conducive to good trade, but there was an increase in green fees at the Golf Club over previous years which Stuart found most encouraging. His spirits were rising. Also, now the new banking arrangements were working and his securities sold to clear the overdraft, the Thorpeness Loan Account stood at £9,596 and he had been paid £4,603 on his First Mortgage Debenture Stock. Work at the Dower House was going ahead, and the minimum rent the Company would ask for it was £200 per annum, excluding rates and taxes, but he was hopeful that the austerity period would not last too long. The last of the Thorpeness rents still owing was promised to be paid by April 1st, so the Season should be able to start well, and with the necessary maintenance and refurbishing done.

Every new management coming in filled Stuart with a feeling of renewed optimism, not to say elation. Mr Euan-Smith (as he wished to be called) took over on February 29th and re-awakened this feeling, and Stuart felt moved (partly for the new Manager's benefit) to put into words once more a re-affirmation of his purpose and hopes. Dating it 29th February 1932, he headed it 'The New Management' and wrote in the Book :

"This Book of Thorpeness is intended not only to be a means of communication between the Creative and the Executive Departments of our Company, but to be a record for future reference of all important events in the development of our Ideal Model Village by the Sea.

We feel that the advent of Mr C. M. Euan-Smith, CBE, MC, (MInst.MM) is an event of the utmost importance and should be recorded in The Book.

Those who have been with us from the first can alone have any idea of the infinite difficulties which have attended the genesis and gradual growth of Thorpeness.

From the very first, our main difficulty in materialising our dream-vision of the place has been finance. The shortness of the necessary funds in the earlier days of our existence made it impossible to secure adequate management. We had to do virtually everything ourselves and naturally found it impossible to obtain efficiency.

The financial position of the Company is today stronger than it has ever been since the hour of its flotation. We are more confident of the ultimate success of the Great Endeavour than we have ever been during the twenty years of its development. Our Company has passed the experimental stage, and, given efficient management, we feel certain that its future growth will be even more phenomenal than its past development."

Stuart concluded by saying they had had four Managing Directors over the twenty years, each one better than the last, but that they had never had one with the experience of Mr Euan-Smith and were looking forward to yet further expansion under his management. Stuart also thanked Mr Bow for standing in so admirably during the 'interregnum'.

This was the last entry of importance he made. He noted sadly that the great Garrett's of Leiston, his old friends, were forced into liquidation by the hard times, and also Gunthorpe's Grocery, among other local names. His dream, he knew, he could never fulfil. He had spent long years in his endeavour against unprecedented odds to create his ideal village. He could not fail, though, to feel pleasure and some satisfaction when he gazed around at the transformation he had achieved. The beautiful Meare, the trees and shrubs, the varied buildings and gardens, the picturesque features - the Windmill and the House in the Clouds - and could only hope that others would continue his work and not let it become just another seaside resort.

His sorrow was that, in struggling to achieve his aim so far, he had spent his inheritance. His "dear mother" (as he always referred to her) had made bequests fairly to everyone. He had nothing but a virtually bankrupt estate and Thorpeness to leave to his young heir, Alexander Stuart. "It grieves me, Sholly," he said "that I can leave you no money at all. But what I am going to do when I've filled the Dower House with my choicest possessions is to leave the house and contents to you."

"Don't worry!" Sholto insisted. "The great thing is for us to get the whole estate onto a profitable footing - and this we can damn well do, even if it means making some drastic changes. Stu will inherit a marvellous estate. It will be a first rate estate. And Thorpeness has a great future."

"I know you will help me, Sholly," Stuart said. "Like my father, you have the business ability ... the gift of organisation ... If only I were not so old ... and I get tired ..."

A few days later, Stuart died in his chair after dinner. He had suffered a severe heart attack. He had been reading a thriller - "Death Tolls the Bell." His funeral, which took place at Aldringham Church on March 12th 1932, was attended by friends from London and from all over the county, while hundreds of people watched as the coffin on a farm wagon passed by. Leading the horses were the two oldest employees on the Sizewell Estate, Daniel Masterton and Albert Tye, who both had over fifty years service to their credit.

The lengthy obituaries referred to G. Stuart Ogilvie as playwright, author and "like his mother, one of the outstanding characters in the County", also as a great patriot, and (what he would have liked best of all) as "the creator of Thorpeness - a Man of Vision."

Chapter Ten

Epilogue

AS YOUNG A. Stuart Ogilvie, the heir, was still at Winchester and about to go up to Oxford in the autumn, his uncle and guardian, Lt. Colonel Sholto S. Ogilvie, DSO, ran Thorpeness and the estates until such time as young Stuart could take over.

Due to his own work in London and his home being in Oxfordshire, Sholto obviously could not do this in the same detailed way as his father had done. First, he decided to ask a well-known London firm of Chartered Accountants to send a partner down to investigate the financial position and system of accountancy, and to give an independent opinion of what action would be appropriate, both for Thorpeness Ltd and Sizewell Estates. This firm's first suggestion - the easiest way out - was to go into liquidation and start again. Sholto was horrified and furious. "What! And not pay our debts?" he roared. "That's just the sort of thing you ruddy accountants would say!"

"And what will you do?" they asked, "with all the Building Societies' loans, the Debentures to be paid, and debts and losses on the farming side?"

"I shall fight," he replied. And they saw there was no doubt that he meant it.

"Or will you sell some land?" they continued. "No, I will not," said Sholto.

After more thought, it was agreed that one of their partners, Mr E. Humphrey, would liaise with the Board on 'ways and means' and be their consultant.

Sholto already had his own ideas. "First, stop the rot," he said. Then, loss-making activities were to be 'plugged', instead of losing money down the drain. Potentially

profit-making ones were to be improved, or run more economically. Sholto made a list. Every corner of the business must be looked into and made a commercial success ("like Marks & Spencers") - or, at least, break even. Mr Euan-Smith was to continue as Managing Director of Thorpeness Ltd. Mr Gilbert West, a London solicitor and friend of the family, took the place of Mr Willett Ram who had resigned after over fifty years service to the Ogilvie family.

A. Stuart Ogilvie at Cliff House in 1930, sitting between his sister Lesley and stepfather Bertie Culver

The start of the "Go as you please balloon race" at the Thorpeness Regatta in 1933

Looking round the rest of the estate, Sholto saw that it was quite impossible for them to run the many farms scattered over the six thousand acres and make a profit under the then depressed state of farming. Paying wages and overheads precluded this. However, a viable living could be made if they were run by small tenant farmers on a reasonable rent. Sholto found there were a number of people keen to take on a farm on their own. Mr S. Lambert, Sizewell Estates Farm Manager, was put in charge of this operation, and he also ran the Home Farm, which they kept, together with the shooting, forestry and other rural matters.

Sizewell Hall was let, furnished, and Scot's Hall and the Dower House were also let - again, at reasonable rents. The result was that the land paid for itself and, for once, a small profit was made. With this, Sholto set up a small poultry farm on a corner of land by Scot's Hall, fit for nothing else, and one of their redundant workers was put in charge. The chickens, ducks and eggs were then sold to The Dolphin, the Golf Club and the Country Club. Orders, too, could be taken for residents.

"It was a good wheeze," Sholto said. "We had our fresh supplies as and when they were wanted. We made a profit for Sizewell Estates which we could put into improvements and building maintenance, pheasant-rearing, etc. - and, vitally, away from the taxman!"

The 1930-s became the hey-day of Thorpeness, looked back on with nostalgia by those who remember it. More people came to Thorpeness, many from abroad. Cheaper tariffs in June and September brought the less affluent with small pre-school age children. More people stayed at The Dolphin for golfing weekends, and Christmas and Easter breaks. In August, the houses could have been let twice over, and gradually a few more were built. People booked from one year to the next, especially for the Regatta. When possible, the Country Club was let for conventions out of season. The first one, for thirty or forty people, was the 'Flat Iron Convention' in October 1932, using also the Great Hall in the Workmen's Club for three days. Weddings and Birthday Parties also took place occasionally. The Old Caddy House was refurbished and let to a Mr and Mrs G. L. Selby as a Day Preparatory School for boys and girls, so as to encourage families of young children to become permanent residents. This flourished until it outgrew the simple premises and the School

moved to a substantial house in Aldeburgh where they could also take in boarders. The Riding School at Beach Farm, run by Colonel Leach and Miss Rosemarie Mason (of the House in the Clouds) was another popular concern.

When Stuart came down from Oxford, Thorpeness to all intents and purposes was booming. The golf course and hard tennis courts had been improved, ten more boats had been purchased for the Meare (to lessen the queues), the Dunes Guest House had come into being and was thriving, beach huts for hire were in constant demand. Treasure hunts, evenings of Housey-Housey, General Knowledge and Quizzes and two Dances a week, run by the Social Secretary, Mr Charles Newham and his wife, were as much part of Thorpeness life as the mini-junior, junior, parent and child, and adult tennis tournaments every week.

The trading figures were remarkably good on all departments. Nevertheless, the Company was not yet financially out of the wood. Profits were being ploughed back in modernising amenities and décor in the houses, in building a large boat-shed for the storing and painting of boats in the winter (previously they had been transported to the thatched barn), in maintenance and building roads, in drainage and water supplies and, of course, work on the Meare, gardens and trees. The Season was still too short. There were not enough permanent residents. During his vacations, Stuart had attended Company meetings and Sholto was keen for him to become conversant with all that was involved in the office, the farms and the running of a large estate.

"As you can see, Stu," he constantly said, "running an estate is not an easy ride! You have to be on top of everything, checking up and always looking ahead and searching for ways of greater efficiency."

It was plain that for the time being there was no way that the Company could support another executive salary, and Stuart himself did not feel ready to take over running the Company as Managing Director. It was decided, therefore, that he should spend a year or so studying elsewhere to widen his horizons. When, after a few months the opportunity came for him to go to South Africa and study business management with a well-known brewery, he jumped at it.

Meanwhile, he had endeared himself to his workers and staff with his easy manner and ready smile, and to the residents and

visitors at Thorpeness as being an amusing party man and a great sport. He had been spare man for Oxford in the boat race (he stood 6ft 2 ins and tipped the scales at 14.5 stone) and had brought the crew down to The Dolphin for a free weekend break (also good for publicity). He was a good shot, and a keen tennis and cricket player, but above all he loved golf. He went out to Johannesburg, joined Chandlers Brewery, met and married Lindsay Daniell, and thoroughly enjoyed life there. Then, in 1939, the Second World War broke out. Stuart immediately joined the South African Army and served in Italy, Ethiopia and North Africa, where he was taken prisoner of war at Tobruk.

Meanwhile, in Thorpeness, the situation was very much a case of history repeating itself. The War Office requisitioned the Country Club and a number of houses, and also Sizewell Hall, the Dower House, and Cliff House. Sea defences were put in along the beach and also some land-mines. Mr Humphrey, who had been made a Director

in 1939, handled all financial arrangements, and Mr West all the legal side. Major Euan-Smith left to take up war work. Fewer people came to Thorpeness than during World War One. Damage to roads and commons was worse, due to tanks, tank traps, and manoeuvres. All along the coast there was a larger military presence with anti-aircraft guns and training exercises. Some enemy bombs fell close to the village, but without loss of life. The Dolphin continued to do good business - better than previously during the winter - due to military visitors, golf (the Club remained open) and short stay holidays.

Sholto had been planning some further expansion, having (in 1936) completed the building of St Mary's Church, as he had promised his father. Now, in addition to his ordinary work as Joint Managing Director of the National Gas Council, he was in command of his local Home Guard at Kidmore End in Oxfordshire, and also a key figure on an Industrial Tribunal. His particular responsibility was to smooth out

Gladys Ogilvie presenting a prize to her son and daughter, Bruce and Elspeth, at the Thorpeness Regatta in 1933. To the left of Bruce - Charles Euan-Smith, Manager of Thorpeness Ltd. from 1932; to the right of Gladys - A. Stuart Ogilvie

labour problems to ensure the constant supply of coal for the gas industry and the other utilities so vital to manufacturing for the war effort.

There was still unrest in the mines, and the communist element was strong. Fear that they might hold the country to ransom again by striking could not be discounted. "Never let trouble fester," Sholto said, and at the hint of unrest he went straight to the spot and spoke not only to the managers and the trade union leaders but to the men themselves. This did not always please the managers, as frequently he had to say "The men have a point. The situation is not right." He then set about suggesting how they could correct it or ameliorate it. Sometimes war conditions made it impossible - or an event had been blown up out of proportion. In either case, with the trade union leaders he went back to the men and explained the reasons. It ended with all feeling they had been fairly treated. In fact, he had been doing this ever since the 1928 General Strike, and in no instance did any real trouble develop. Once when he returned home from a tough assignment in Scotland, he recounted with some amusement how, after the meetings were over and all was settled, he was having a drink with some of the trade union representatives and men when one said "Tell us, for why d'ye wear those silly spats?" Sholto said he replied with great emphasis "Because I've got bloody cold feet!" They roared with laughter and said "Och, that's all reet then! When you first came in we thocht you were jist anither bletherin' toff."

After the War, Stuart returned and, on May 14th 1945, took over his estates as Managing Director (and was now known as the Captain) with his uncle and guardian as Chairman (known always as the Colonel). Stuart was on a modest salary, with bonus arrangements. Sholto never took any remuneration.

The following year, Sholto retired from business in London and moved from Oxfordshire to the Tea House, Sizewell. This,

he renamed Ness House (as he was tired of people coming up off the beach wanting teas). Stuart and Lindsay took over the Dower House. By 1947, with the soldiers gone, Thorpeness was more or less back in full swing. The Country Club with all its social events in action and - the joy of Stuart's heart - the Golf Club. He never liked to miss a day's play. Lindsay was made a Director of Thorpeness Ltd, and also Bruce, Sholto's second son, who had lost a leg in North Africa while an officer in the Grenadier Guards and was now studying to be a doctor. Glen, Sholto's eldest son, a Flight Lieutenant in the R.A.F., sadly had been killed in action in 1940.

As the years went on, Sholto's health was deteriorating and Stuart took over entirely. He favoured a casual approach. Meetings were rarely called, and orders were given by word of mouth. There were no officially recorded Directors' Meetings in 1956 and 1957. Mr Gilbert West had resigned, and Mr E. Humphrey had retired to Bournemouth and seldom came up. In March 1958 it was felt that the Company must expand and acquire more land from Sizewell Estates, and in particular a limited development around Sizewell Gap to bring in more revenue, not only in the summer but for permanent homes for expanding Leiston and for workers from the Central Electricity Generating Board who were building the Sizewell "A" Magnox Nuclear Power Station just north of the Gap. Selling this land had brought a boost to Sizewell Estates, and the contractors, Taylor Woodrow, had also leased Sizewell Hall for their staff meantime. It was then that Sholto reminded Stuart that now he had a son and heir (aged 10) and three daughters, he should make the estate over to him (as his grandfather had when he was young) to avoid death duties as "none of us know when we shall pop off." Sholto always said that Stuart gave a charming smile and said "Yes, Nunky, I must do that," when he suggested anything - and doubtless thought that "old Nunky"

*St. Mary's
Church, 1936*

made a bit of a fuss about things as he was managing perfectly well and was still able to get on the golf course by 11 o'clock most mornings.

In May 1960, a Directors' Meeting was held (the first since 1958) followed by another in December, when Sholto once again urged Stuart to make the Company and the estate over to Glen. "Yes, Nunky," said the easy-going heir, "I must do that *now*."

In March 1961, in his 77th year, Sholto died after a series of strokes. His funeral service, which he had planned himself, was held at St Mary's Church, Thorpeness, followed by his burial in the family plot at Aldringham. The Colonel was a very popular man on the estate, always fair and ready to listen - like his father but much less "awesome" - and always ready for a joke, with a wonderful line of "whimsy." The men knew, too, that once having given a command, the Colonel made sure that it was carried out. They could not 'flannel' their way out of it with him, and he told them as much, over a drink at The Dolphin.

In 1971, Stuart's son Glencairn Stuart was appointed a Director of Thorpeness Ltd. On 12th September 1972, Stuart suddenly dropped dead of a massive coronary on his beloved Golf Course - typically, in the middle of a joke. He was not quite fifty-eight. The village was shocked. He had been the easiest of bosses, more often than not it was "just carry on as before.." or "I know you'll do the right thing..." when asked about a job. It is true that sometimes both workers and residents took advantage of his good nature, but visitors loved him because he joined in all the sporting events and was a jovial host at the bar of both the Golf Club and the Country Club.

When Glen took over the complex and difficult job of managing this diverse estate of approximately six and a half thousand acres, he was twenty-three and still at Writtle Agricultural College, with no business experience or wise old "Nunky" to guide him. Unfortunately, his father, full of good intentions and bonhomie to the end, had only made over the estate to him a year or two earlier (when he had a heart "warning" and had been told by his doctor to moderate his way of living) and the seven years which would have avoided death duties had not elapsed. Land prices at that time were abnormally high, even for marginal land, and

Glen found he had death duties on his hands for well over a million pounds, a number of debts and financial commitments, and little cash. The estate was also overmanned, badly maintained, and sadly run down.

The Auditors advised that in order to find the sort of money required there was no alternative but to put Thorpeness Ltd into voluntary liquidation and sell its assets. A London Liquidator was therefore appointed. Glen was, anyway, primarily interested in Sizewell Estates and farming. Furthermore, Stuart had disentailed Thorpeness Ltd so that his three daughters would share in Thorpeness Ltd. Glen decided, however, to buy the Meare for himself at Probate. The Golf Club, the Country Club and The Dolphin were sold, likewise the houses which did not house his employees. Scot's Hall was also sold, and the bird sanctuary at Minsmere (started by Sholto) which the R.S.P.B. was glad to purchase for between a quarter and half a million, including extra land over which he once shot. Many people who had rented or leased houses for years were glad to buy them freehold - often paying well below the market value. Some properties were immediately spruced up; others, perhaps slow to sell or bought for occasional cheap holidays or summer letting, fell into a sadly neglected state - a far cry from the band-box look and colourful gardens of G. Stuart Ogilvie.

In 1987, during the hurricane of October 16th, Glen lost thousands of trees and several woods. He gave up his shooting syndicate, and rearing birds - at least for a while. He now proceeds as a farmer, with his wife Jenny (née Duggan). They have a daughter and four sons, and they live at Hawsell's Farm (in Margaret Ogilvie's day the home of William Kemp, the builder, the grandfather of Graeme).

The Dower House and Sizewell Hall are both let, and Cliff House, which was running successfully as a caravan site, is sold.

Glen had taken most of his farms back under his control, with a Manager, but, with farming going through difficult times, he started contracting land out and sold the Westleton Walks. In 1991 he decided to put 1300 acres of the coastal land from south of Minsmere to Thorpeness on the market for approximately a million pounds and only retain about 1000 acres near his home to farm himself. Since then, Glen has virtually sold the estate, and now contracts his fields out. He, too, much enjoys golf, also travel.

Thorpeness itself is a Conservation Village - one of the few 'purpose-built'. It will never, therefore, be allowed to stray far from its Creator's original concept. More houses have been built - sadly, not to the Designer's plan, and some that should never have been allowed to be built in Thorpeness at all. However, most fit in well, and people coming back who remember "the Old Days" are always delighted to find it so little changed. The Regatta and the fireworks still go on as before (as Glen kept the Meare himself) and the tennis tournaments continue (thanks to the late Mrs Alyson Bell who bought and re-started the Country Club). Many other old Thorpenessians also have decided to retire here and watch their grandchildren exploring the magic of the Meare, the fort and the crocodile, as they and their parents did. Even most of the boats are the same ones, kept beautifully painted. 1988 saw the 75th Anniversary of the First Children's Regatta - and a few Thorpenessians could "remember it well", while there were a number on the landing-stage who had not missed a Regatta (except during the Wars) for fifty or sixty years or more. Some family rivalries are now into their third and even their fourth generation.

G. Stuart Ogilvie would like this. His dream has survived two World Wars and endless tribulation. He may have lost the solid reality of a fortune but in its place he achieved his great wish and has bequeathed us all the wider and more durable gift of beauty and lasting pleasure - the materialisation of the burning, fragile vision of *One Man's Dream*.